“Rule of Thumb”

Published by
Vintage Reprint Service,
Lodge Wood Farm, Hawkeridge,
Westbury, Wilts BA13 4LA.

www.stationaryenginebooks.co.uk.

E-mail: Enginbooks@aol.com

ISBN 978-0-9554625-0-4

Printed by
Ralph Allen Press
1 Locksbrook Court
Locksbrook Road
Bath BA1 3EN

Artwork & design by Les Gates-Mutton

The author (left) and Lord Braybrooke with Polar Star. (Photo by Hon. Mrs Emma Carboni, daughter of Lord Braybrooke and goddaughter of David Curwen).

Foreword

David Curwen has been a close friend and adviser on all things mechanical for over forty years. In the early 1960s I realised that I might be able to build a miniature railway which would be a viable proposition and at the same time provide entertainment for visitors to Audley End House. Accordingly, I wrote to the firm of Bassett-Lowke who immediately put me in touch with David, who at that time was running the firm Curwen & Newbery in Devizes, Wiltshire. We soon became good friends and David provided enormous encouragement and help with the whole project. The success of our Railway is very much due to his knowledge of running railways, and his ability to design and build hard-working and robust locomotives so necessary for a commercial operation. In March 1963 my father asked me who would pick up the bill if the Railway was a failure, but thanks to David's expertise its future was assured.

We still meet regularly and David spends two or three nights with us each year. We both love trains and always will!

***Lord Braybrooke*.**

Publisher's note

When I called to see David Curwen towards the end of 2005 it was to collect a Petter hot-bulb marine engine that I loaned him for research purposes in the early 1970s. "Ah, just the chap," he said when I arrived, and pointing to what I subsequently realised was the manuscript of a proposed autobiography lying on the table, continued, "You've published a few of your own books, how do I publish this?" For a number of years David had been putting together a fascinating collection of humorous anecdotes, written in easy-to-read fashion, beginning with his school days and running through his working career which included the maintaining of generating plant, steam vehicles for road use, and the construction of sundry miniature railway locomotives.

At the time I was in the process of completing my own book *The Lister CS Story* and certainly wasn't looking for another project, so I agreed to make enquiries with regard to locating a suitable publisher. However, looking through David's collection of early photographs I realised some would be in need of what would nowadays be rather delicately called 'computer enhancement' so I agreed to undertake that particular task. During my next visit David asked if I could illustrate the section dealing with generating plant. He then followed up with, "If we could get the text written onto a CD disc, maybe you could read it through?" Gradually I was becoming the publisher of his autobiography by default! However *"Rule of Thumb"* is a fascinating story of engineering in a bygone age, of a type we won't see again, explained in a light-hearted and modest manner. I am honoured to have played a small part in publishing David Curwen's memoirs. I hope you enjoy reading them.

David W.Edgington 2006.

****

Author's note

"Rule of Thumb" has been written, over a period of around five years, entirely from memory as I have never been one to make notes or write a diary. Although I have tried to ensure the various facts, statistics and names mentioned are correct I would like apologise in advance should I happen to have made the odd mistake—being in my 90s I am sure you will bear with me. Thank you.

I would also like to especially thank David Edgington because without his help this book would never have been published.

Acknowledgements

Lord Braybrooke, William & Maggie Willans, Alan Thomsett, Eric Brain, Joyce Mountain and David Edgington. Plus the many people who have assisted in so many ways over the years to make this story possible.

Life is like a hard metal; however hard the task is, don't take too long weighing it up, just start cutting, you will get the odd sharp bit of swarf and you may even tread on it in your bare feet but just carry on cutting it!

David Curwen

Chapter 1

Born with steam in my veins!

I entered this world on November 30th 1913, being born in Sydenham in Kent. My father was one of a large Victorian family, four sons and three daughters. Initially they were quite wealthy having business in the city, but with good living, and so many of them, there was little left when I arrived on the scene. The Curwen family is quite ancient coming from Westmorland and Cumberland, now Cumbria, and I have records dating back a thousand years. However we only need to go back far enough to establish exactly what engendered my life-long interest in steam power.

It all started a very long time ago. My grandfather on my mother's side was a naval engineer. He was one of the first engineers at the time when steam was supplanting sail. I remember him as a rather fierce old man, but he would draw me the loveliest sketches of ships' insides. He was very much of a character as illustrated by his personal diaries which fortunately are still in existence in possession of my cousin. The beauties and attributes of his many lady friends throughout the world were always described in a code which my cousin finally managed to solve!

The other major thing that must have been an influence was my father who would take me in my pram to the railings of our nearest station to watch the trains go by. At the time we lived at Sydenham but this came to an end when he volunteered for the army; I imagine this to have been 1915.

After the war we bought a house in Kent, about 35 miles from London and within ten minutes walk of the station. Using the South Eastern & Chatham Railway my father went to the City every day, while I was able climb a tree and watch the steam trains cross a small three arch viaduct. I was always rather disappointed that the only passenger locos were of 4-4-0 wheel configuration, no longer the beautiful brass domed Wainwrights, while goods trains were 0-6-0. I don't think anything heavier was ever used along that line.

My father bought this house after he was demobbed at the end of the First World War and sold it after the Second World War had started. The garden had been landscaped by its first owner, and there were nice banks instead of the block walls shown here. In the foreground a tennis court and shrubbery, now cut down. Nightingales nested here every year and May evenings were sheer heaven.

We had four acres of garden. Two around the house, which had been landscaped by an actress who had built a similar house for her mother and had a very early private phone in her bedroom – the instrument was still on the wall.

The other half of the garden consisted of an orchard and a patch of rough ground, a right of way to the railway station passed between the two halves. Tall hedges made it private. All father had to do was make a ten minute walk out of the back gate, across a meadow skirting a wood, then through a corn field and finally over a stile which led almost on to the up platform.

Some years later they started to build the main coast to London road, via Maidstone, and in the holidays I could watch an everlasting stream of ballast lorries running past the bottom of our garden. Sentinels, Fodens, and a few ex-army petrol Atkinsons, all in clouds of dust as the road had not been tarmacked at that time. Otherwise it was a quiet country spot, the nightingales nested every year in the bushes. I often wonder what it is like now with Brands Hatch only two miles up this road?

I was sent away to boarding school at Westgate on Sea for the statutory three terms and in the Christmas term always posted off my sixpence for the Bassett Lowke railway catalogue. Gradually the steam bug began to bite but little did I realise that years later I should build for Bassett Lowke and have a loco listed in their catalogue!

I started of course with "0" gauge, first Hornby, but at long last I was promised a steam engine for Christmas. Christmas Eve and night, sleep was impossible, the moon streaming through my window – when would morning come? When it finally arrived, it was a blue 0-4-0 tender engine, priced in the catalogue as £2.2.0. Looking back on it from 2006 the price paid was a considerable sum of money in those days, more than a week's wages for many senior men. Anyhow it went, and it went well, methylated spirit fired, along a straight track down a long room, all along the edge of the carpet. What would the health and safety people say now? But we were taught and learned to be careful and were trusted to be thus.

Time passed and I had a small line in the garden, and by

In the Christmas term at boarding school, I posted off six pence for a Bassett-Lowke catalogue; little did I realise that years later one of my locomotives would adorn this venerable catalogue!

saving and saving at last had the five guineas required to buy a Basssett-Lowke Mogul in L.M.S. Red. This was clockwork, why I cannot think, but at least it kept its colour, which was usually burnt off after a few runs with the steam engines. Replicas are now made under steam at £600 plus.

A young man passes through many phases in his hobbies, and as time went on, I became interested in such things

In a mad moment of nostalgia I decided to have an engine built for me in memory of the first Bassett-Lowke locomotive I ever had in steam---back in the late 1920s. It was a 0-4-0 Caledonian in 2 1/2 inch gauge just like this one which now adorns my bedroom!

BASSETT-LOWKE LTD

SCALE MODEL

L.M.S. Railway Company's
2-6-0 Type Locomotive. No. 13000.

Electrically Driven. Steam Driven. Gauge No. 1.
British Make.

13000

UNTIL recent years the only "Mogul," 2-6-0 engines running on the whole of the L.M.S. system were a series of five, built some years ago for the Caledonian Railway. The London, Midland & Scottish locomotives authorities have at last, however, succumbed to the attraction of this type of locomotive, for mixed traffic service, and have designed the standard type which forms the subject of our model The general lines made familiar in the Horwich designs of the late Lancashire and Yorkshire Railway have been followed, and large numbers of these engines have been

After some judicious saving I had enough to send £5-5s (five guineas in those days!) in order to acquire a L.M.S. 2-6-0 Mogul Class in clockwork—it seems inconceivable that I didn't specify steam power!

as motor cycles and cars. First of all it was of course motor cycles especially as I was still at school. I had now left my prep school and gone to Kings Canterbury. For £12 I had bought a Levis two-stroke of about 250cc, and as you can imagine, my parents needed a lot of persuading!

It was a reliable machine, with only about 50 mph. as top speed. As I bought it during the term I had to find storage for it which I did at the main garage in Canterbury. On half holidays I would go down and ride it round the car park and in between the cars, I seem to recall this area was also the garage car wash.

One day this nearly had an abrupt ending. A yellow Austin pulled up outside and at once I recognized it as the Headmaster's car so I beat a very hasty retreat. It was considerate of him to have such an easily recognisable yellow car!

Academically I was a disaster, partly due to ill health. In the winter terms I spent two weeks in class and two weeks in the school sanatorium alternately, mostly suffering from heavy colds. Kent could be a very cold place in winter in those days of the late 1920's.

One hard winter everything froze, including our cubicle washing water, having no heat in the dormitories tends harden you up! The school was very decent in this cold snap, a half holiday every day so that one could toboggan, skate and generally enjoy the fun. We had a prep school attached to the main school, Milner Court, and it had a small lake which was well frozen. I went skating, mostly on my bottom, but it was still great fun.

All my various illnesses landed me in the senior sanatorium under charming Sister English. She must have persuaded my parents that I required my tonsils removing so in due course I was plonked on a table in one of the small wards while the school doctor did the job. He was a real character with black beard rather like James Robertson Justice and drove a black Rolls Royce. He was assigned to do the job so anaesthetic was administered by placing a mask over my mouth and nose and the ether or chloroform, or whatever, being sprinkled on the gauze. My wife will not believe it, but it was so. I can remember waking in the night and wondering if the soreness would ever go away. Pain killer was ice given me to suck. We, in the 21st century, don't know how lucky we are.

Sister English was a very kind soul and well known in the local Canterbury society. She used to take me out for runs in one of her friend's A-type Ford saloon, the friend being the daughter of one of the Cathedral Deans.

Nursing staff consisted of nurses-cum-housemaids. Sister English was giving a dinner party and I can recall one of the maids telling me that she didn't know how they could eat the pheasant they were preparing, "Crawling with maggots they be". I bet they were good, but I must say that I have a preference for modern freezers and game not quite so high. After remaining in the same form for what seemed like too many terms, it was decided that schooling had no great future for me and I was moved on to a crammer in a large house near our home in Fawkham.

For all that, I appreciated Kings School–and 'appreciate' is a fairer description than 'like'; it was an experience that did me good, character building if you like. One learned to live with, and by, others.

Never tell tales, stand by your friends and the school. I fagged for the Captain of Games; Cook was his name and of wealthy parents no doubt as I had a credit of five shillings per week at the canteen. As tea or supper consisted of bread, butter and jam, the odd tin of baked beans and a sausage, this came in handy at times.

The dining hall was a lofty building with a very high beamed wooden ceiling, and every now and again, if one had a butter pat left over, in warm weather a bent knife could be induced to flick it up to the ceiling, where it would stick until the weather got really warm!

In the morning at breakfast, the Housemaster on duty sat at the head of the table, and if by chance one was late, you had to apologise as you passed him. Good for the soul, in those days "manners maketh man" was the byword.

When I think of the present Nanny State I wonder how we survived, but you were taught to be responsible. I was interested in engineering and proposed to become an engineer. A Science master, Mr.Goodburn, who was a great character told me, at my request, how to make Blue Prints, and I went to the local chemist and bought the necessary chemicals, one of which was Prussic Acid, deadly, but no one doubted that one would be sensible and careful.

This same Science Master would spend a lot of the lesson telling his class that he was a "self-made man", which was true so good luck to him. I took extra lessons with him in his house in the Cathedral precincts. He had a Red Indian wife, or so it seemed to me at the time.

We had one very amusing accident which could have been far more serious than it was. I was in a chemistry class with Mr.Goodburn, who apart from his usual talk on being a self made man, was demonstrating the dangers of phosphorus, which has to be kept underwater as it fires immediately it is in the open air and subject to a small amount of heat. I was sitting on one side and noticed that he was about to cut the stick with a knife which he had forgotten that he had recently held in a Bunsen flame. The inevitable happened; there was a flash, showers of sparks and acrid smoke. We had to beat a hasty retreat while everything was doused in water!

I was passing the laboratory after dark and looked in. The lab attendant said "come and see, I've got to watch this all night". Every crack and pinhole in the desk was glowing with little spots of light like glow worms. However all was well and it didn't catch fire.

We could get permission to do extra work in the lab on wet half holidays, but had to state which experiment we planned to do. I was in one afternoon, with about four others, when my neighbour said he was going to try and make some friction matches, not of course the experiment he was supposed to be doing. I didn't pay much attention and he began to grind up his mixture in a pestle and mortar, suddenly there was a hell of a bang; the pestle missed me but ended up in a fume cabinet having broken the glass, while a small boy walked around in a daze, saying, "whatever happened, whatever happened?" We had to take him to the sanatorium for first aid. His hands were bandaged for several days, fortunately his eyes were O.K.

I never liked the Officers' Training Corps. very much, both marching and drill were not my cup of tea–the only part I excelled in was shooting. I was a crack shot and earned a rifle badge on my tunic arm. We had one field day on the down land above the town, with 5 rounds of blanks. These downs had a lot of sheep and some enterprising lads found that the sheep's pellets were pretty good at repelling the enemy! I took cover in gorse bushes of all places, the gorse, not at ideal habitat!

Puttees of course were leg coverings, any one of you ever tried tying these on? Breeches to army boots, tape must finish outside the knees, and you had to do them up so very tight or they would come down, a black mark!

How one envied the officer, and wondered why the army did not dress the troops thus, in the end of course they did.

After leaving Kings, I went to a nearby 'crammer' in Hartley called the Old Downs,(cram or crammers are specialized schools that train their students to meet particular goals, most commonly to pass the entrance examinations of high schools or universities.), making the trip of a couple of miles each day by motorcycle. One of the pupils was a mischievous French lad, and many a time, when I went to get my Levis from the garage, he had pinched it for the afternoon. This ended when he got picked up by the local Bobby for speeding at nearly 50 miles an hour! Evidence was thus, "I 'eard the roar of engines, I saw a motor cycle a comin' and when I looked again it were gone".

One most wonderful thing that came about was a friendship I struck up. The owner of The Old Downs, a Mr Strickland, found out I was interested in railways and things mechanical. He said, you must get in touch with Geoffrey Barrett, son of Captain Barrett R.N., he is very keen on railways. I did this as they only lived in Meopham in the next village, and a friendship resulted lasting until the present time.

The only other thing of interest at the Old Downs was their electric light plant driven by an open crank engine of 15 or 20 hp with a wobbly flywheel which, although firmly fixed, ran out of true.

Chapter 2

A brief introduction to internal combusion

An uncle of mine had an Electrical Engineering business in Victoria Street, London with branches in Bristol, Beckenham and a works at Leatherhead. He was a friend of De Havilland, and was familiar with various Clubs in London which had electric lighting installations. Other customers had plant in some of the larger private houses while even larger plant was used in industrial circles. My cousin, Bob Curwen, was a few years older than me and we were good friends. As he said many years later, we should have gone into business together, I wish we had, we would certainly have got on well and maybe could have made a good living. 'Maybe' is the right word as both he and I were more interested in the fun of the work rather than the money.

One day we hatched a crazy scheme of making a motor boat and sailing it round the coast of Britain. We built a small boat and one day, when his Leatherhead works was on holiday, he and I went down to make the shafts etc in the works. We had a twin Douglas Motor Cycle engine, but needed all the drive and prop shafts. We both set to using several of the lathes, and worked non stop till the early hours of the morning. When we returned to Bob's home in Beckenham, a very irate Uncle Charles, who had also been pestered by my parents while looking for us, was somewhat displeased! All before the days of mobile telephones–only very crude hand-sets existed, ours had the phone number of Fawkham 12, whereas nowadays we have to remember 10 to 15 digit numbers!

I spent the night in Beckenham and rode home the next day, I can't remember if it was on the Levis or if by then I had bought a Scott and sidecar.

Before buying the Scott I unfortunately managed to prang the Levis. I was riding home with my sister on the pillion round a winding lane in the next village of Hartley. As I was about to round a sharp bend, a butterfly alighted on my knee, I think it was a Red Admiral, for one moment my attention was disturbed and a Mrs. King of Hartley chose this moment to come round the bend–and wham! I ended up gazing at her through her mighty Austin 12 windscreen. My sister was in tears and the poor Levis had a very crumpled front wheel and bent front forks. No one was hurt as we were both only travelling at about 25 mph. How we got the Levis home, I can't remember but I expect by pushing it!
As I had the Levis when I was still at school, it was laid up during the terms and used to take me a day to start it when I got back. It was many years later, in fact not long ago, that I found it was petrol deterioration and if I had drained it out and filled with fresh fuel everything would have been O.K.

This meant another bike and Bob, my cousin, suggested we visit specialist motor cycle dealer Pride & Clarke the next Sunday, which we did and bought a Scott and sidecar for £15. Bob drove us down to Beckenham, where he lived, and I took it on from there. My first ride with a sidecar was to put it mildly, a bit of a thrill, if that is the right word for a very scary ride. When you turn to the left toward the sidecar it lifts off the ground, the other way it digs in, so to speak. This was easy to deal with but needed a bit of handling in order to get used to it, furthermore the Maidstone main road on a Sunday evening in summer had two lines of fast moving traffic with people returning from the coast, and they tended to pinch you in the one lane left to you. However I made it with grateful thanks.

Although we lived only 35 miles from London, there was no electricity outside the village. All our lighting was provided by oil lamps or candles. The Aladdin mantle lamp gave a good light but if you didn't get the setting right it developed a black blob hanging from the mantle and you had to turn it down to get this off. So being a budding young engineer I thought I could do something about this lack of lighting. I talked it over with Bob and he agreed to get me all the wiring, switches, lamp holders etc. from his firm and I would go about getting a dynamo and engine etc. My first efforts were pretty dismal. We had decided on 25 volts so Bob found me a small dynamo and I rigged up the old Levis engine and although the Levis had a flywheel it still wasn't substantial enough.

While we are on the subject of motor cycles we might as well go through them all. Next then was the Scott, a twin cylinder two-stroke water cooled, these were lovely machines. There were two types, the Squirrel and the deluxe Flying Squirrel. The Squirrel, which was my bike, had a vertical oval tank with the saddle just behind and a small gap rather like a lady's bicycle between the tank and the honeycomb radiator with the engine beneath giving a very low centre of gravity, good for cornering! The Flying Squirrel had a horizontal tank from the saddle to the radiator, the tank filling the gap, rather streamlining. Mine was a two speed model, fairly old, a rocking pedal, back for first and forward for top. Unfortunately whoever had fitted the Torpedo Ali sidecar had not altered the sprockets to suit, meaning it would do 48 mph in bottom, but only 49 mph in top! The chap that I finally sold it to took the sidecar off and then managed 70 mph with ease; I wish I had done it!

There was one small defect in that the kick-start was located by the rear wheel and worked the opposite way to the usual. Every now and again it slipped when you gave it a hefty kick, giving your ankle and knee a wallop!

Of course the lighting was acetylene. You filled the container with Carbide and water above, set the water drip, opened the lamp and applied a match. On occasions it would blow out in bad weather and this was a problem, you opened the front and tried to strike your match and when successful there was usually a pretty fair bang. With this system the light was very bright and people could see you coming but conversely you couldn't see where you were going as it gave no useful beam. However traffic was so very light it didn't seem to matter.

I was doing evening classes at Gravesend Technical School, five miles away and I remember when coming home one night the rear chain came off. I had a spare link but no spring clip. The only answer was to thread back one of the Bowden clutch or throttle cables so I judiciously cut off a 2 inch length and wired on the link. It got me home! One had a pretty good tool kit and it was essential to learn to use it, even on a very wet and windy night and you always carried a torch!

I had reached the age of 18 by now and my mother and godmother, who lived with us, thought it might be a nice idea to have a small car. We always hired a private car, a Trojan owned by a Mrs. Darling whose sister-in-law was an American film star named Estelle Winwood who incidentally, only died in 1984 aged 101. Anyway, Mrs Darling had this Trojan and I was allowed to lean over and steer it! The Trojan was a reliable vehicle with solid rubber tyres and a twin cylinder two stroke engine, started by heaving up a lever on the right hand side of the driver, but it worked. My mother, possibly somewhat inadvisably, accepted an offer to go to Thirsk and back with a friend who had another one of these.

Anyway, this is a bit beside the point so back to looking for a suitable small car. We heard that a doctor in the next village, Hartley, had an Austin 7 hp Chummy for sale for about £65, so I went up with the money to collect it.

Although my total experience of driving amounted to leaning across Mrs Darling and steering the old Trojan, I duly climbed in the Austin Chummy while the doctor showed me the controls. He looked a bit troubled as I drove away but my motorcycling had taught me how to use a clutch, accelerator and brake. Furthermore as the brakes took 25 to 50 yards to stop the car, it didn't make any difference!

For many years I had a licence with a note, "Licensed before April 1934" on it, well before the first Driving Tests. The next few days were spent "getting the hang of it". We kept the Austin Chummy for several years, but after I started my apprenticeship I went back to a motor cycle on economy grounds. A local policeman had a pretty ancient TT Sunbeam, a long stroke machine of about 1924 vintage, which he had kept it in wonderful condition. It was very well made, all the chains were in oil baths, it had electric lighting and although it had a slow speed engine it was very fast. It had one fault and that was the main rear brake. There was a V-pulley of large diameter on the rear wheel, rather like a veteran motor-cycle belt drive pulley, and a wedge shaped brake block was pushed into the V-pulley. Braking was alright in dry weather, but in rain nothing happened for a second and you automatically pressed harder with the inevitable happening, it suddenly jammed and you were in a good skid and usually came off.

I was trying the machine out one day, as the front fork springing seemed to need adjustment. We hit a pothole and the bike went into a speed wobble which ended in the usual way. We turned over and slid along the road with me underneath. I remember thinking that I never knew bones sparked before, as my elbow was getting very sore, and my shoes were scattered along the road. I could not lift it off and had to wait for an errand boy to pass and give me a hand.

Of course you didn't have crash helmets and padded jackets in those days, just a cap or leather flying helmet and a sports jacket—which this crash had left in ribbons. News travelled fast even in the 1930's. This spill happened about a mile from home yet by the time I arrived, my dear mother, who was a placid soul, said "I am glad to see you dear. I just had a telephone call from Mrs Matchet (the Vicar's wife) who said she was so horrified to hear you had been killed on your motor cycle!"

When we had the Austin Chummy, the only trouble I had was when out one day, driving too fast as usual, I met a large car coming the other way in a narrow road. There was an almighty thump as I grazed by and in the mirror I saw a wing see-sawing in the road. I got out of the car in fear and trembling, but all I could find was a small dent in the back wing. The wing in the road belonged to the passing Armstrong Siddeley, the owner of which happened to be our family doctor. He was a little cross and called on my father later that evening. I had to eat humble pie while they sat drinking whisky; life is a little unfair sometimes.

Through all this time Geoffrey Barrett spent a lot of time with me at weekends. He was studying very hard for his engineering degrees etc. but he used to take time out and nip over in his father's large maroon Austin 16 as he hadn't a motor cycle of his own. Anyway, there was a Mr Myers who was a funny sort of chap with a workshop behind his house in Hartley. He had an open crank stationary engine-driven electric light plant and a lathe, plus heaps of useful things lying around, such as an old twin Enfield motor cycle. In the workshop, Myers carried out various odd jobs for the local community like charging radio batteries. I think his wife was the earner. She went to town every day working on the very leftwing newspaper, the *Daily Worker* I think it was, they were way-out Marxists. She was no beauty, rather the opposite. My father told me that on the morning train, she went by the name of Mary Pickford!

Anyhow to cut a long story short, Geoffrey and I bought the old twin Enfield motorcycle for about £4 and took it to my home.

We worked on it for a number of weekends but never extracted as much as a peep from it even though we checked everything. In the end we took it back and Myers gave us most of our money back! I remember that we even took off the magneto to have it tested by the local cycle-cum-motor engineer in Longfield Village, a very fat chap who rejoiced in the name of Mr. Sims. His method of testing a magneto was to hold the HT lead in his fingers, twist the shaft and if he got a shock it was O.K.!

He also had an old Model T Ford which I recall watching him swing the handle in an attempt to start it. Nothing happened so he removed the radiator cap and dropped in a penny saying he knew he had forgotten something. Of course it fired and went first turn, much to amazement of his audience. He was a bit of a joker!

An old carpenter named Gillam lived next door to Mr Sims. He had done some work for our house, and I was asked by my parents to call with a message. It was a bit of a shock to a boy when the door was opened and I went in; there was a coffin propped against the wall. The old man just said "I'll need it one day soon"!

In the end Geoffrey Barrett bought a little round tank B.S.A. 250 cc, certainly not a sporting or fast machine but very reliable. BSA (Birmingham Small Arms) made good little engines. I bought an air cooled B.S.A. stationary engine for a 7¼ inch loco in the 1960's. We also bought mass-produced Briggs & Stratton engines at the same time for boat drives, they were also good engines.

Going back to the early thirties, Geoffrey and I started to make a Metropolitan 'Growler' loco. I still have one bolt from this effort but we didn't get very far as Geoffrey was studying very hard and his father kept him at it. He of course, passed all his exams and went to Messrs. Ricardo & Co and then on to Shell working in its engineering research departments. He spent some time in the oilfields in the Middle East. I, on the other hand, could not be classed as an academic and I loved practical work and just wanted to get on with the job in hand! Through Geoffrey I met a very good motor engineer named Hugh Forsythe who had a small garage in Meopham, he had a wonderful reputation. My father, who knew absolutely nothing about mechanical things, persuaded the garage owner to take me on as apprentice.

I have often thought that this was a mistake as I should have gone to Halls of Dartford, or Avelings or Shorts at Rochester. But on the whole, having come across many of these apprentices from large firms, I feel that maybe my training, where from day one I just had to do all manner of work, was not such a bad thing, although this way climbing the ladder of life took much longer.

We have to go back to my efforts to light my parents' home at East Dene, Fawkham, by electricity. My cousin Bob Curwen had got me all the wire, switches, junction boxes etc from his firm Buchanan & Curwen, while I rummaged around and got a small dynamo and linked it up to the previously mentioned Levis engine. The end result wasn't much good, so I went over to local garage owner Hugh Forsythe, who had a small very well made scooter engine which I bought and duly fixed up. However, much like the Levis this wasn't much better. It didn't like running for long periods and the light flickered very badly. To improve this I sorted out an old cast iron pulley which I bolted onto the flywheel but then I had starting problems. I decided to take it over to Hugh and asked him to see what he could do with it. A few days later I went to collect it and found Hugh in bed, furthermore the garage roof had several holes in it! It transpired that he had started it alright, but it went off at a terrific speed and the pulley which I had fitted had burst, resulting in a piece hitting him thus laying him up for a couple of weeks! These days there would have been a large claim for compensation and Health & Safety issues, but instead this forged what was to become a long friendship and the start of my joining him in the garage.

It was quite obvious that my lighting effort so far was a failure, so I started to look for something more substantial, settling on an old Chevrolet lorry engine of all things. As four-cylinders were not required I took out two of them and fixed the engine up on a concrete stand in a concrete block shed which I built especially, my first effort with cement, sand and blocks. We had a government scrap merchant in an old chicken farm in the next village and 'old Brown' was a constant source of building material and scrap tools etc.

The Chevrolet engine was another failure, it never did start. By this time I was getting a complex! It had to be better luck next time.

Opposite Geoffrey's house in Meopham, there was a rather scruffy garage and mechanic's workshop, and while poking around in there, I found a good heavy Fairbanks Morse hopper-cooled farm engine of about 4 to 5 hp and also a good sized 100 volt D.C. motor which I was assured would charge 25 volt batteries when run as a dynamo, and it did...

But first, having got all this junk home, starting the engine was the next item on the agenda. First I must describe the Fairbanks Morse. It had about a 5 inch bore, two good hefty flywheels of about 30 inches diameter while the well of the engine housed the paraffin tank. It was of course an open crank construction. It had a gear driven low tension magneto supplying an igniter plug which can only be described as a large set of points on a flange casting, the points being inside the cylinder and actuated via a trip mechanism and spring. This was operated by the lever

With Geoffrey Barrett, I adapted a heavy-duty Fairbanks Morse farm engine for lighting plant duties at my parent's house at Fawkham. Various intricate modifications enabled it to operate unattended for periods of around six hours while using paraffin as fuel made it economical to use.

which worked the exhaust valve and was controlled by the governor working on a 'hit-and-miss' basis. When the engine reached its governed speed, the lever held the exhaust valve open, so the tune the engine played was 'bonk, bonk, bonk, shu, shu, bonk, bonk, shu, shu' altogether quite mesmerising!

The first task was to get an initial 'bonk, bonk' out of the engine so I took the igniter out and cleaned it well and gave Geoffrey a ring. He arranged to come over on Saturday and give me a hand, promising to bring a 'persuader' in the form of a little bottle of ether he could borrow from the laboratory!

Well, Saturday arrived and we anxiously stood by the engine. I swung the handle while Geoffrey applied the ether and, lo and behold, the 'bonk, bonk, bonks' were plentiful but without any 'shu, shu, shus' so we were forced to retreat from the engine shed. We hadn't thought to bolt it down which was turning into a problem as it proceeded to waltz around the floor. However this only lasted a minute or two before it died down and stopped. Even so, we decided there and then that this would be the engine but the lighting plant required certain modifications prior to setting it up.

A hopper cooled farm engine was generally used for short runs and not intended for the several hours required for charging house batteries, a task that could run into a twelve hour operating period in the winter. Furthermore on a farm there was always a farm hand to top up the hopper with water, replenish the paraffin tank and oil cups, clean the igniter contacts which seemed to soot up quickly—on this engine anyway.

So to work, the first job was to blank off the hopper, fit inlet and outlet pipes and a cooling tank. Most of the tools were manual in those days as electric drills were not everyday household pieces of kit. So this one simple task took a lot of hassle with much toil, sweat, hand drilling and filing, I've never liked filing since, but it was done in the end.

An essential modification involved replacing the antiquated low-tension ignition system by removing the igniter and fabricating an adapter plate to take a high tension spark plug. Locating a suitable high tension magneto was easy thanks to an abundance of scrap motor-cycle engines lying around—I regret not hoarding up a couple of hundred! The example seen here shows an H.T. conversion on a smaller Fairbanks Morse.

The next unreliable part was the contact spark arrangement. In those days there was an abundance of single cylinder motor cycle H.T. magnetos around so one of these was obtained and fitted in place of the old low tension magneto. The contact igniter was removed, and a steel plate cut, drilled with a bench hand-drill, and tapped with a gas thread as used on Ford Model T car plugs at this time. This modification worked fine, in fact I feel sure it was generally adopted by other engineers who had experience with that archaic L.T. ignition system.

Next was the carburettor. This was just a right angled casting with a needle valve, taking its fuel from the shallow tank in the engine base. No float chamber, so when running the engine, you had to re-adjust as the fuel got lower. Again motor cycles came to the aid. A carburettor with a float chamber was fitted and a two gallon gravity tank on the shed wall to supply about 8 to 10 hours running.

The last job was to extend the cylinder oiling capacity, so an oil tank with a visible drip-feed was fitted on the wall with pipes running to the cylinder oil pipe, and larger big end and main bearing oil caps. With all this done, 6 hours running with no attendance was possible. The dynamo quite happily gave 5-10 amp 25 volts with the engine running quite slowly. I made my own switchboard, with a nice little mercury cut-out. We handled mercury as an every day material for such contacts, these were days without hordes of do-gooders and Health & Safety officers milling around; you just knew what you were doing, if you didn't, you took steps to find out!

This set-up lit a fair sized house for some years, using 12 gallons of paraffin per week costing about 7½ d old money per gallon. There was a rather superior fuel called Shell Spark at the same price, it was some by-product of refining and seemed to have a good petrol content included. Anyway we chose to use it and it was quite satisfactory and the plant itself provided light for several years.

The batteries were 14 glass jars of open type, about 12 inches high and 6 inches by 8 inches. I forget where I bought them, but probably the aforementioned garage. I emptied the acid into a Carboy, and brought it home as and when required in the poor little Austin Chummy.

By this time I had acquired my first lathe, a 3½ inch Drummond, a good sturdy machine which I thought a good deal better than the Myford. Although Drummond lathes were unique in having a round bed, I chose and preferred, the conventional type. The Guildford based company, Drummond Bros., Ltd., also, for a short time, made a 3 hp stationary engine called 'Willing Worker' which could be supplied with a portable power-saw or just as a basic engine. Until recently I've used a lathe dating back to 1913, a good cast-iron job unlike the modern light-weight machines. I was lucky because my parents had a workshop built for me in the garden; it was all wood, erected on brick piers. Size-wise it was about 18 x 10 feet with wooden floor and 2-foot windows–all at the vast cost of £18.

Chapter 3

Maintaining generating plant

When I finally joined Hugh Forsythe as an apprentice, I found one of the jobs which we did from time to time was in connection with electric light plants for houses of medium to larger sizes in the lonely country areas and they usually had voltages of mainly 25, 50 or 100. Most of the villages already had mains electricity. The garage itself had a 25 volt system run by a very ancient horizontal petrol engine. It looked almost a home-made job, and of course there was a fair trade in charging 2 volt wireless batteries. This plant was succeeded by a 'proper engine' in the form of a Lister and dynamo on a channel bed plate. I can't remember where it came from, but the old engine shed was too small for it so it was installed in a corner of the main workshop from where it fortunately gave off a little heat. The building was just corrugated iron with no lagging or heater; it was so cold that I suffered from terrible chilblains! Nobody would work under such conditions nowadays.

The Lister, being a petrol engine, tended to be expensive to run as it was in operation most of the day, in fact I recall it used around six gallons each day. Imagine that nowadays, six gallons a day! Anyhow back in the 1930's, it was also a costly exercise so we ran it on paraffin without fitting any form of vaporiser. It didn't like this one little bit, as it was too well cooled, so objected by belching a form of a black greasy exhaust residue which spilled over into the silencer, which was an old galvanised tank sunk into the ground. One day this caught fire and burned spectacularly for several days – but sadly even then it didn't heat the bitterly cold workshop!

We supplied and serviced all sorts of plants, the smallest but very effective was the 50 volt Stuart Turner, driven by a small 2 or 3 hp two-stroke. These plants were incredibly reliable and were directly coupled running at quite a high speed. I got to know the Henley on Thames-based firm of Stuart Turner fairly well after the war when I started making locomotives as it carried out a lot of casting work for me, I dealt with a very helpful Mr Bence. The main work at the time was War Government Contracts which had to be completed even though the engines were no longer needed; they ended up going into Government surplus. Stuarts wanted to get on with post-war work but through usual Government stupidity they were forced to complete the War Contracts for equipment no longer required!

At the factory I was told another amusing story involving government stupidity. Stuart Turner always tried to persuade the Navy to buy its small engines, but with no luck. Why? Because the Navy only had instruction books dealing with the operation of four-stroke cycle engines so any form of two-stroke was out of the question!

When degaussing against mines at sea became very urgent the Government needed small generating sets for shipboard duties so the M.O.D. bought a few Stuart electric plants. The resulting comment, "these are excellent, why have we never bought them before?"

But generating sets at remote houses provided a great deal of business at that time. One, at a location I can't recall, had a superb example running a horizontally enclosed Crossley engine which someone had finished in a chocolate brown, as opposed to the normal green. There were two automatics,

We serviced a pair of automatic lighting plants, a twin-cylinder Kohler and a single cylinder Delco—the latter requiring six gallons of petrol (to be delivered) per week. Delco sets, like the one shown here, were extremely popular though quite costly to run if frequently used.

An Amanco I went to service always sat in an inch of water with oil floating on the top. Engines, such as this one, were cobbled up just to keep them running, and surprisingly they ran for years. Note the positioning of the chain-driven H.T. magneto! The carburettor, fuel tank and silencer are also additions.

a Kohler twin water cooled and a Delco single air-cooled. They both started up when you switched a light on. We used to supply 6 gallons of petrol per week for the Delco. The generating of electricity wasn't always a cheap option! At Stanstead in Kent, in the next village were two other types of lighting set. General Lance had an acetylene gas plant, while another house had a petrol gas plant. We supplied special petrol for the latter which had a small air compressor or pump which passed air through the petrol, the gas was then collected in a small gas holder.

This small air compressor was run by a wonderful system of ropes and pulleys attached to a tall tree, you wound it up and it gradually worked down. I was told that a heavy wind would vary the pressure and make the lights flicker!

Near the garage, on a lane opposite, lived a retired planter and family. The wife was a bit of a pain, always referring to, "When we were in Madeira my dear". I did not like going to repair this plant which was driven by a little Amanco Hired Man situated in a cramped outhouse, the floor of which was always an inch under water with oil floating on top. Nobody ever bothered to clean anything.

Back to Stanstead where a brewer named Mr.Biggs lived at Wrotham Hill, a lovely house set back on the escarpment with a wonderful view. He had a very nice 100 volt plant which I think might well have been an Armstrong Whitworth. When he finally went onto the mains electricity, Hugh and I bought this plant and built a new block shed for it. It drove the dynamo by belt and you started the engine with a handle which connected with a pin in the crankshaft, over which there was a guard. One day when Hugh was starting it, he forgot to put the guard over the pin and when he leaned across to switch over from petrol to paraffin his overalls got caught on the pin which stripped most of his clothes off, throwing him in a corner. It took six weeks in bed to get over it. These old stationary engines can be unkind; you need to keep your guard up, literally!

Now we come to the engine which I really enjoyed. Situated near Wrotham Hill was a mansion, Trosley Towers, owned by Sir Philip Waterlow, the printer of bank notes. The family had another house so while the Towers remained empty, a caretaker and his wife would look after it. The agent for the estate was General Lance whose wife was a member of the Waterlow family. We were asked to run the plant to supply the mansion with light as there were no longer chauffeurs and gardeners employed. There was a magnificent engine house in the middle of a lot of substantial outbuildings well away from the house and situated in the woods.

The engine house was a fine building with a quarry tiled floor, the water and main paraffin storage tanks were in the next room, a tap in the engine shed filled the main working fuel tank which was I suppose held about 25 gallons.

The engine itself was a vast open-crank Crossley with hot bulb ignition, an extremely early example. From memory it had about a 12 inch bore with a flywheel of about 6 feet in diameter with the lower portion sunk into the floor. An outrigger bearing on a pedestal was situated by the wall near a window while a belt of about 6 inches in width drove a large 110 volt dynamo. I cannot remember its charging rate but it must have been something over 25 amps.

There was a fine black polished slate switchboard and a desk and chair for the attendant. Leading off from the engine house was the battery room containing 52 large glass cells

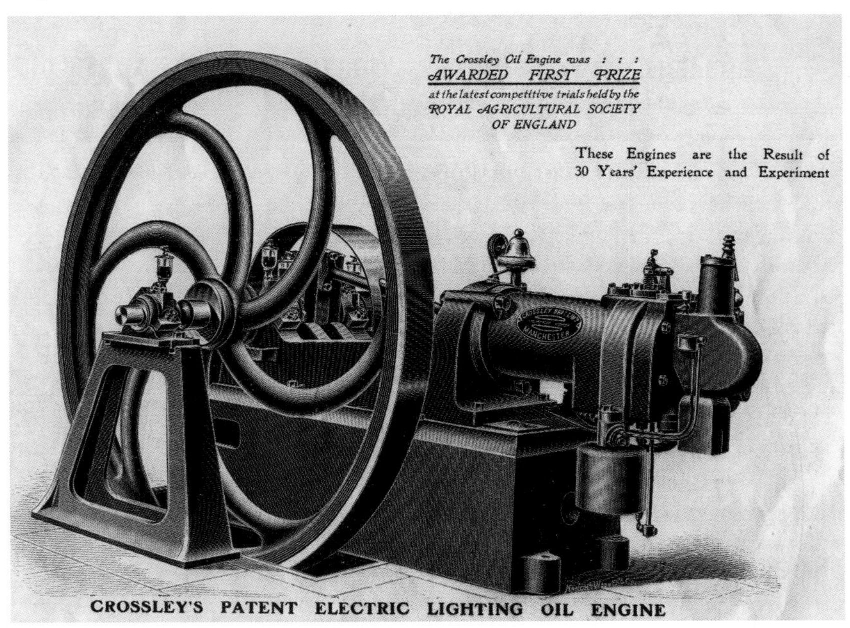

The Trosley Towers engine was a huge piece of fire and brimstone when you could finally start it, but once running, thumped away endlessly having a soporific effect on any onlooker mesmerised by its motion. Its output was around 40 hp and it looked rather like the one in this contemporary illustration.

about 30 inches long x 18 inches wide by 24 inches deep all placed on wooden beams on the floor. The amount of lighting required was negligible so we only had to charge about once a fortnight, but we were called in times of emergency. These emergency visits came about due to insufficient use of the plant, plus the fact that it was fairly old. The lead plates were starting to warp, and in doing so would often push out the side of a jar. We had to bore and blank the cell out with a hefty wire, being particularly careful as the floor was swimming in sulphuric acid. Fortunately it didn't happen too often as there were fuses on the cells consisting of a strip of about 1/8 inch thick lead about an inch wide. Fortunately I only had to go once!

The governor of the engine was no longer reliable, so I was detailed to look after it all the time it ran. In the winter this was a fine job, the engine shed became wonderfully warm and I stayed there until the cells were fully charged and gassing well and the hydrometer well up. This was fine, but starting the engine was another matter. The task required two of us and could easily take an hour.

As I have said, the ignition was hot bulb, an enormous cast iron bulb the size of a small man's head attached to the cylinder head. A giant primus type blow- lamp had to be lit first and brought up to the required heat, and then it was applied to the bulb. When the bulb was considered hot enough one of us, usually me, had the onerous task of swinging the flywheel. This meant climbing on the spokes, grabbing a wire fixed to one spoke, jumping off and heaving like hell from the ground.

As I said this was of course my job! The other chap had a lever about 2 ft. long which was pivoted in such a way that when he gave it a heave it worked the fuel pump and injected a charge of paraffin into the hot bulb. If we were lucky, the engine fired at that point. It was too large, and the compression too great to get it over top dead centre, so you swung it back and forth, until finally the momentum was enough for it to rotate. Being the boy, I would heave on the flywheel spokes against each compression while Hugh, the pump operator, would give it a burst at the appropriate time. It certainly made the floor tremble. I recall watching the connecting rod, which was the thickness of a man's arm, quiver like a cane if Hugh was a bit in advance with his squirt! Finally you would go to the switchboard and put in the main switch. The engine would immediately take up the load and the belt would make a pleasant slapping noise.

Once, when a fuse blew and the huge machine started to speed up, I just made a dash for the fuel tap and was relieved to hear the momentum begin to falter.

This was the same noise you used to hear in the old days of threshing with a traction engine. There had to be a fair distance between the pulleys for a good belt grip, and the belt was from the rim of the flywheel to a small dynamo pulley, I can't remember what the engine revs were, but it was fairly slow by modern standards, 150-250 rpm maybe. A wonderful soothing rhythm, inclined to send one to sleep as the day wore on and the warmth took hold.

My main job while remaining with the engine during the day was to keep the oil cups and glasses full. This was fine except for the oiler on the outrigger bearing which nowadays would have carried a Health & Safety warning. To reach this I had to flatten myself against the wall and walk crabwise with arm and oil can extended before me. With the steady 'shoo, shoo, shoo', the whirring flywheel behind me and the draught blowing close to the back of my overalls, a very sudden and gory death would stare me in the face, about twice a day. I often wondered why the installers had not thought to put the oiler in an extension pipe but in those days the odd estate worker was probably expendable! At the end of the day I would shut it all down, lock the doors and go out into the rather spooky wood outside, collect my motor cycle and ride home. I didn't drink in those days, but a visit to the Vigo pub near the estate would have been nice. I've since made up for it!

As a mere matter of interest, I drove up to this area on 30th November 1936, the night the Crystal Palace burned down. The glow was easily seen for many miles, I often wondered if this was done on purpose. War clouds were gathering and the Palace was a landmark in SW1.

Returning again to the garage where car repairs were done, and what a variety of cars could be seen in those days. Much more individuality than today and many of them had particular faults that went with each make, but most were simple compared to the present day car.

For instance anyone owning a Morris Oxford or a Cowley was wise to carry a couple of spare axle shafts as the end of a shaft had a tendency to twist off. It was an easy job to take the old shaft out, but it was easier to take the other out and use a small rod to push out the broken section.

The clutch on these cars had a plate full of holes with corks in them; they ran in oil and now and again had to be replaced.

The charging and starting was all done by a dynamo starter, driven by an inverted tooth chain, no grinding noise when starting. If the chain broke you had to take off a right angled steel plate covering the front of the gearbox and side of the sump, and it was a terrible job afterwards to get the corner oil-tight. Headlamp dipping was managed by the lamps being set on a cross bracket which swivelled, operated by a lever controlled by the driver. This gave me an idea for my Austin 7 Chummy. Dipping lights meant going on to a dim light, which wasn't much help, so I rigged up my own headlamps on a pivoting bar and worked it with a Bowden motorcycle cable. Everything was fine until one night on my way home, the end came off the cable and the headlights shot upwards!

A chap called Mr Hewlett had a Clyno, he was a friend of the family who had the previously mentioned petro-gas lighting plant at Fairseat. One of our jobs was to repaint the Clyno for him as it spent most of its time garaged. I always thought the Clyno was actually a better family car that the Morris, it was very simple and reliable but for some reason they did not achieve a great following and like many others went to the wall. The firm went bankrupt in 1929 with the assets being purchased by Birmingham based R.H.Collier, although I recall having to collect spares from somewhere near Vauxhall Bridge in London.

Although there was an abundance of makes of car, each type seemed to have some main fault and you needed to be pretty knowledgeable as well as versatile in order to cope with them. It was so different from the present day when garages and motor dealers tend to specialize in just one brand. A good example of this happened a while back when on my way to Saffron Walden in my thirty-five year old Jaguar XJ6. Suddenly the throttle failed to respond. Being an automatic with a big engine I was able to crawl to the nearest large garage–a Renault or Peugeot agent. I went to the foreman and asked for a mechanic to have a look. He said he'd be glad to fix it, but after half an hour nothing had happened. When I asked why there was a delay he said they only repaired Renault and Peugeot so had to call in a specialist!

In the end a chap came in a van, found it was a cable clamp loose and tightened it in 3 minutes. £20 to pay! Of course one could have done it oneself, but you can't sit in the car and work the throttle and look at the engine at the same time.

Back to the early 1930's, the little Singers at that time had back axle trouble. S.K.F. bearings mounting the crown wheel had sheet metal raised cages holding the ball bearings. These invariably chewed up, rivets came out and the metal broke. The answer was to fit Ransome and Marles bearings with bronze machined cages.

The £100 Ford 8 saloon had a weak back axle with a tendency to break teeth resulting in a new crown wheel and pinion.

Most cars needed decarbonising every 10-20 thousand miles, and valve life was quite short. A combination of World War Two technology from America combined with leaded petrol seemed to remedy these problems.

So many types of car, General Lance had an Essex, a large American car and then a Standard of about 16 hp. One of his sons had an M.G. while the other had a Singer Sports. One day the General came to the garage to see Hugh. "Forsythe" he said (as military hierarchy tended to do) "I was in London with my son's M.G. when it made a terrible noise in the engine, would not go properly, took it to the garage, they said crankshaft's broken, don't believe it, would you check."

So I was sent to have a look. Although the sump was off it was possible to start the engine which would run slowly, but the slightest increase in speed and it made a terrible noise! The shaft had broken in the centre, and the break was a jagged one, so the two halves mated together at tick over but tried to go their own ways at anything above this speed.

The General was a nice chap, when you could cope with his gruffness, and due to a little over-indulgence had lost his licence. I was often detailed to drive him up to his regimental luncheons and then bring him home after. At this time he had the large Standard 16. Fetching him back one day, he snoozed off in the back, so I drove carefully and not too fast. When we got out of the suburbs onto the open road, a voice from the back said, "David my boy, this isn't a 30 mile limit you know". So I whipped it up to 70 and he returned happily to sleep.

The local greengrocer had a large and ancient Dodge which he toured the village with his wares. He was an awkward customer. He came in one day with a puncture– if I remember correctly the wheels were of the split rim type. I duly repaired same and he came and collected the old battle wagon. Next afternoon he was in again with a moan, "that tyre has gone flat again". After he had gone I attended to it and guess what I found inside? I had not been able to find that favourite pair of pliers all day!

A certain lady, a Miss Helen Nogate, was a friend of Miss Forsythe who kept house for Hugh. She had a pretty little Triumph saloon, with a sort of glossy fabric body, nowadays one would call it mock leather, it was light fawn and the pride of her life. It was in for servicing one day and parked near a large tool board we had on the wall. Hugh was on a ladder painting in the tool shapes, so that you knew where everything was—I think they were referred to as 'shadow-boards'. Suddenly he knocked the white paint-pot off the ladder. It hit the floor and the paint flew up in the air covering the Triumph. It took him many hours to clean the poor little car and get the paint out of all the cracks!

I was sent up to Sidcup one day to collect an old 10 hp De Dion-Bouton which belonged to an old friend and colleague of Hugh's. At that time it was quite an old car, and I suspect it had been bought for £10 or less– you could get a good second-hand car for around £5, no M.O.T. certificates needed in those days. It is worth bearing in mind that 50 mph was pretty fast and most traffic cruised along at around 30-40 mph. I duly collected the De Dion which had a long bonnet somewhat restricting the view from the driving seat. I came across some road works, so I pulled myself up by the steering wheel in order to see where to stop. There was an almighty crack and the rim broke off in my hands! Fortunately two spokes still remained and I used these to steer the rest of the way home where I received a good wigging for being careless. I never liked this car, it had a honeycomb radiator, and a starting handle that came very close, and after skinning my knuckles on this, I liked the car even less. Nowadays starting handles are not required but in the old days a year was a good life for a battery. The last car I had with a handle was a 1954 R type Bentley, but it wasn't a lot of use as it was too difficult to turn!

Working with Hugh provided a real insight to early motor car engineering. There were plenty of old Austin cars around, and while the 4-cylinder 12 hp was good, the six cylinder not so. One had to be careful when having the crankshafts reground as sometimes they would break when in use; they seemed too weak and were strained when used in slow speed engines.

At an old farm house in Meopham there lived a nice chap Mr Baugh and his wife. He was an early property dealer, buying estates for next to nothing, and then splitting them up. He had an old Singer Tourer while a brother had an Armstrong Siddeley. The brother had spent a lot of time in Canada and returned with a large fur coat which he liked to wear– in the winter he tended to look more like a bear than a man. The Singer wasn't quite the car for seeing expensive clients so Baugh asked Hugh to try and find something more in keeping for a property developer. So he went up to London and located a magnificent Daimler Double Six sleeve valve open tourer at Stratstones of Mayfair. Baugh turned it down and then proceeded to go and buy it direct, thus doing poor old Hugh out of any commission. Hugh didn't bear a grudge especially as it turned out to be a terrible car to start. We got in touch with Daimler and they suggested we fit a Ki-gas priming system as tried on early aircraft, but to no avail. It was always a difficult starter so was only used for special trips, but when it went it was super, terribly quiet, and with its fluid flywheel you could get out and walk beside it. It also looked the part in a wonderful, light grey with a blue line on the typical Daimler type bonnet, blue upholstery and the wheels were all chrome plated. It had been a young man's toy until his money ran out! I think Mr Baugh paid £200 for it. The engine was very clean with a chrome plated exhaust manifold to match the wheels!

For some time we had a twin cylinder air cooled Rover as a garage car, it was pretty crude with an unreliable shaft driven dynamo. I don't think it had a self starter as we always used the handle but with its two very large cylinders it had a kick like a camel and woe betide you if you didn't let go at the right moment, the handle could swing round and break the back of your hand. Although it had magneto ignition, its main failing was the gravity tank mounted on the scuttle. It fed a carburettor located on the inlet pipe above the cylinders and if you forgot to turn the petrol off at night, and the float wasn't well seated, you could arrive in the morning to find one cylinder full with petrol. This meant removing the spark plug and turning the engine to pump out a cylinder full of petrol, which was a terrible waste in terms of time and fuel. In a bad temper one day I was sent out to do a job I didn't like and cornered far too fast lifting the Rover onto two wheels, it almost went over. A frightening experience!

In a nearby village lived a customer named Happenstal who had a little Humber tourer of ancient vintage which he brought in for odd repairs. On one occasion we had given it a tune-up and taken it back to his house. A few days later an angry Mr.Happenstal telephoned sounding somewhat annoyed saying, "the damn car won't start come and see to it, you repaired it". I replied asking, "Have you turned the petrol on, sir?" (It had a gravity tank, petrol tap under the dash). "Of course I have I'm not a fool". So out I went making the 5 mile trip, turned the petrol on and started the car. Rather than saying "you silly old fool" I erred on the side of discretion preferring, "I've made a small adjustment, you'll find it fine now!"

Just up the road from the garage lived the Bolster family. Many of you will remember John Bolster the well known author and T.V. motoring commentator. The family had a Frazer Nash, a wonderful sports car with chain drive to the back axle; they were also building their 'Cycle Car' destined to become the famous *Bloody Mary*. John Bolster used to belt around in this car making one hell of a lot of noise to which the police either turned a blind eye or didn't know about it!

We did however have a very good country policeman named P.C.Martin who would call at the garage, usually at time when I had been driving too fast, or noisily through the village. He tended to have a discreet word with Hugh asking him to give me a quiet warning. This was proper policing, he knew everyone, and everything that went on in the neighbourhood, and in this way it was a pretty law abiding village, much more effective than the present day system. Nowadays the village policeman has disappeared, consequently policemen no longer know the locals, and furthermore they tend to upset people by being so unfriendly.

I remember riding home one day in fog as dense as pea-soup, my motor-bike producing a steady "pom, pom, pom" while crawling along at 5 mph. Suddenly there was a loud guffaw and there in the gloom was P.C. Martin, "You've had it tonight you young rascal, haven't you!"

Good old Martin, he retired and of all the coincidences, I was walking down Regent Street in Swindon in 1942, as by that time I was working at Shorts Brothers, and walked slap bang into P.C. Martin, who was doing war duty there! What an amazing coincidence.

Sadly times were about to change. It was during the recession, money was tight but even so we still had plenty of work at the garage. Hugh had a very good reputation but both he and his sister were devoting more time to 'good works' plus a fair amount to do with the church. No doubt they thought I was quite capable of running the business, but the point missed was the fact that a small business tends to revolve around one person and customers expect to deal with this person. I was finding that our better class of customer like Mr Briggs, the Brewer, General Lance, etc., after calling two or three times and not finding Hugh in attendance were giving it up as a bad job. After all in their eyes I was just the garage boy, so as the work began to tail off I could see where it was going to end.

So it was time to cut my losses and move on—but where? Most new cars we had sold had usually been of the Standard make coming from a very good dealer in Chatham named Russell's Garage. So I paid Mr. Russell a visit and he took me on.

Russell's Garage was in a large warehouse building, backing onto the river Medway. Half was divided into two storeys, the top of which was the office and workshop reached with a car lift. They generated their own electricity and Mr. Russell, with an eye for showmanship, had mounted a pair of lovely horizontal open crank engines on a raised portion at the back. They were both diesel engines, of either Crossley or Blackstone make (I cannot recall which) but they were in full view and ran extremely well. The smallest of the pair ran in the daytime while the larger ran all night. We had a terrific clientele with much evening work as we were situated near the Chatham theatre. One of our chaps was a parking expert and tightly packed in as many cars as possible for the theatre clientele, after the show he diligently extricated each car as required.

I had been in the workshop about a year when Mr. Russell asked me to do a turn in his coachworks, in another part of town. I was under the impression he felt that the two chaps already working there were swinging the lead. The only trouble with bodywork in those days was the hand rubbing down with "wet and dry". After about 6 months there he asked me to join the salesman, a chap called Hawkins. He was a good salesman and with an appropriate stock of slightly doubtful stories but he had one extraordinary accomplishment–driving along he recognised any passing customer simply by the registration number of the car. I often got personal jobs for Mr. and Mrs. Russell, such as driving daughter Madge to her school in Bexhill. I often wondered if Mr. Russell had an ulterior motive to this as he had no son to take over the garage.

We did a lot of work for the Naval officers in Chatham, hence the good array of sports and unusual cars. The owner of one particular Aero Morgan three wheeler crashed and unfortunately killed himself. The Aero Morgan was a fast little car, but they could turn over and the steering always seemed very flimsy to me.

We were also agents for BSA motor cycles, and had a Gold Star in the showroom. This was some machine, and although I never rode it, we started it from time to time, and the power was certainly there.

As a salesman I wasn't one of the best! I managed to sell a few second hand cars, but of course the pick of the sales and the new cars fell to Hawkins being manager.

One thing was a bit of an eye opener to me, and that was the fact that pampered cars, owned often by ladies who used them about town for shopping, and kept them well, should have been first class buys second-hand, but this wasn't always the case. I remember a nice little B.S.A. in 'very clean' order, as sales people say, which ran a big end on almost my first run in it.! When repaired I did actually sell that one, it went to our local rector's wife at Fawkham. The difference in bearings was sorted out during the war, the Americans had found that, having thick white metal, instead of lasting a long time did not distribute the heat and therefore melted (ran). The modern practice of very thin shell bearings got over this problem, and of course the oil pressures are much higher now.

One day an Austin Seven Saloon was taken in part exchange, I suppose it was about 1929 vintage. Anyway I bought it, for the magnificent sum of £7.10s. (£7-50p) and did many miles in it until well into the war years; its registration number was RW39. A number like that would be worth a great deal of money today!

Some of the cars of those days were really memorable. I had the opportunity to drive a large number as I was loaned a car each day for the journey home, and while some were really nice, others had such little value they ended up at the scrapyard.

I remember being loaned an old Sunbeam saloon with a large fabric body. It really was a lovely car, the six cylinder engine was so well balanced that it was smooth and silent with no rubber mountings to stop vibration, they simply weren't needed. I think the crankshaft was machined and balanced from a single billet of steel. What a car, but it went for scrap as it had no value whatsoever.

As Russell's Garage was an agent for Standard, we sold and serviced a large number of this make so it made a welcome change for us to see a front wheel drive Citroen, a very advanced car at the time.

It's funny to think that in those days, you overhauled a car engine completely, took it out of the car, stripped it down, rebored the cylinders, reground the crankshaft, scraped in the bearings and reassembled the whole thing. Now, well, a car does 100,000 miles easily and you change for another!

I remember that behind Hugh's garage was a large house and park owned by a Mr.Foa who had been closely connected with the Rothschilds. He was elderly and the only car he ever drove was some veteran two-cylinder type, I can't recall the make, maybe it was a Renault or De Dion Bouton. It had lovely buttoned leather seats, all very high up, and he and his elderly wife would perch high up in bath-chair type seats and potter around. His friend, General Wigram, had a very old Humber that we re-painted and worked on when required; this was a nice little car which, I seem to recall, had an overhead inlet and side exhaust layout rather like a 1954 Bentley I once owned.

Chapter 4

Time for a change

At Russell's Garage I was getting the feeling that I needed a change, as well as a little more money, furthermore I'd always wanted to get into manufacturing. Short Brothers, seaplane works, always seemed very busy with well paid staff, so I went along to their employment office, only to be told they were not taking on any more staff at the present time.

Often in life it is not what you know but who you know. As it happened I had previously returned a car, after a repair, to one of the Superintendents, so I decided to go and see him one Saturday afternoon. On his doorstep I related my tale to which he kindly advised, "Go and report to Employment department Monday at 11 o'clock." I did as I was bid and – straight in with no bother at all! Report to Mr Baines in No 3 Shop!

On reporting I was given a drawing to mark out on a sheet, and asked how I would make it, and after about an hour the supervisor came around and said "O.K., your rate is one shilling, four pence and a half-penny per hour (old money), here is a slip to give to the office, report to Mr Wenham your chargehand tomorrow at eight, with your tools. I found I was lucky as I was started at a penny above the going rate.

I entered Rochester based aircraft builder Short Brothers around 1935. Among aircraft being built at the time were the huge Short Sunderland and "Empire" flying boats. No 3 shop was the main erecting area and it was a vast corrugated building with a high roof and very large doors; outside was a road and a slipway into the river for launching the flying boats.

There was a Singapore flying boat in for repair, and the current production was an order for Empire flying boats, both for Imperial Airways and Qantas Airways while the far end of No 3 Shop was given over to Sunderland building for the R.A.F. Although I did a little work on the Sunderland, my main job revolved around various tasks on Empire flying boats. It wasn't long before I was given a routine set of jobs; I made up all the pulley brackets and fairleads for the tank level indicators called Televel Gauges. This was a peculiar system, but I suppose it was designed to eliminate positioning any electrics near fuel. There was a row of gauges, six in all, 3 for each wing, with each gauge having a wing screw outside on its face, for operation by the Flight Engineer. The wing screw worked a copper Bowden cable, copper cable and copper sheathing. Inside the tank a split aluminium tube ran from top to bottom and a float worked up and down this with the fuel level. This float had a finger fixed to it.. The end of the Bowden cable was fixed to the top of the tube and there was a pointed copper slug which fitted the inside of the tube. The flight engineer would turn the wing screw on the gauge until the slug stopped at the float and that showed on the gauge the quantity of fuel in the tank.

The fairleads that I mentioned before ran from the pilot's cockpit under the floor to take the wires which controlled the fuel tank cocks, these wires finally ran over pulley wheels set in light alloy brackets. I had to make up these pulley brackets and install them in the aircraft. One of these I hated fitting, it was the top centre assembly which was fitted to the rear upper main beam in the centre section.

The vast Sunderland flying boat was, for its immense size, extremely impressive. Its construction comprised a deep hull with wings and engines set high up on the fuselage, well away from the water. The hull was designed with a single step in order to break the suction of the water, making take-off easier. Opening the throttles of the four Bristol Pegasus air-cooled radial engines created a terrific draught!

The centre section comprised of four T-section main beams, to which the ends of the four taper wing beams were fitted each side with fish plates, these of course were the main stress members carrying the weight of the hull section in the wing area.

Fitting this pulley assembly meant drilling the main beams so no mistake was allowed, all reamed holes were inspected. So this tended to be a mental strain until it was passed and stamped. All drilling was done with a Desoutter Mighty Atom air drill, no electrics in the shop, everything being pneumatic.

Whilst on the subject of these tank gauges, a special job cropped up a few days after war was declared. An Empire flying boat in the last stages of construction was in the Barge yard ready for launch and delivery. For some reason best known to the design staff, a very urgent modification was required. This was to remove all the Televel cables and substitute duralumin (one of the earliest types of age-hardened aluminium alloys) alloy pipe in place of the Bowden flexible outer cable, so a gang of us were called up to do this quickly with day and night working. To the best of my memory we worked all day Friday and all Friday night, all Saturday, and crawled home Saturday night. I used to drop a chap off on my way home, travelling in my Austin 7 Saloon. This time he had to keep prodding me to keep me awake! We came in Sunday morning, worked all day and all night and finished the job. But when the inspectors came and tried it Monday morning it didn't work! The inner cable would not go round the bends in the solid duralumin pipe, it worked with the outer Bowden sheath because it was made of copper wire like a spring, coated with braided material outside, but the inside was like a fixed ball bearing, the cable working over the inner tops of the copper coils. So, "Stop work on this", and a couple of hours after, "Take it all out and replace originals!" I was paid for 100 hours that week, a record £8 15s in old money!!

While we were working in No 3 Shop, there was a grand clean up one day as Royalty were paying a visit. George VI, Queen Elizabeth and the two daughters, our present Queen and the late Princess Margaret made a grand tour passing just a few feet from us. My most striking memory was the wonderful complexion of our venerable old Queen Mother.

The Barge Yard I just referred to was the finishing yard for engine testing before flight. It had actually been a Barge Yard in the days before Shorts had it, large Thames barges had been built there. It was just outside the Main Gates, and the flying boats were launched down the slipway outside No 3 Shop, towed to the Barge Slip, and hauled up. The road to the works ran behind the yard and the other side of the road was a steep grass field, and further along, under this steep bank, almost a cliff, nestled the works. It was a favourite spot for Sailors, and others, to take their girl friends on summer evenings. The Engine gang had a great sense of humour – when trying out the engines; they would suddenly open the throttles causing a terrific draught from four Bristol Pegasus engines guaranteeing the lift of many a skirt, much to everyone's pleasure.

The flying boats were taken from the Barge Yard and moored on the other side of the river. For any further adjustments, a fitter was taken out by the works' launch. I was taken out one afternoon and appeared to have been forgotten. It was quite eerie with dusk coming on and water slapping against the hull. I had to stay put until the men came out to turn on the mooring lights for the night.

That was a particularly bad winter, causing the Medway to start to freeze over so a launch had to be employed to circle the flying boats all the time to stop any damage to the hulls. During this very bad weather, No 3 shop was terrible; it was so cold we had to wear overcoats as the hot-air heating system never worked. They brought in 40-gallon drums in which were lit coke fires but the fumes were terrible giving many of us bad throats. Furthermore the technicians thought the smoke was affecting the anodising coating on the hulls, so out went the fires and we all became colder! No men would stand this today, but good jobs were not easy to come by.

One very difficult job I had was forming the side of the throttle boxes. These were a difficult shape with reverse sharp curves, and the problem was to stop splitting the metal when hammering them over the formers, constant annealing in the large salt baths was a necessity.

I remember well a tall blunt rather gruff Geordie chap who had a heart of gold. He saw my difficulties and showed me what to do, we became friends, and I remember him telling me he had come south to get work. "George", he said, "you have no idea what a year on the dole does for you."

He lived on the outskirts of Rochester and as I passed his door I often dropped him home. One Christmas on our midday break up he said "you must come in and have a drink and a piece of the wife's Christmas cake". This I did, but the half glass of neat whisky – "You'll have it neat, of course" – nearly burnt my guts out! At home I dropped my lunch box while getting out of the car and I can tell you it certainly took a lot of picking up!

I was always known as 'George', and this came about in a funny way. I had a chargehand named Wenham, and one day I heard him giving instructions to a chap to pass a job on to me – "Give it to George" – "Who is George, Mr Wenham?" – "You know George, for God's sake, the chap with the la-di-da voice!"

One of the troubles we had was the supply of standard A.G.S. parts (Aircraft General Stores). They supplied standard pulleys, small nuts and bolts, Simmonds lock nuts, and I suppose the demand was such, that there was not enough to go round, this meant that my under-bench was quite full of uncompleted jobs, just waiting for some small bit or piece. Not a very happy state of affairs.

Our gang had a miserable tea boy who probably came from one of the slums of Chatham. He never laughed except on one memorable occasion when it would have been better to have cried. Some men were working on the roof, which was a good way up, and one unfortunate chap fell through and onto the electric bus-bars where he lay jumping about getting a shock. At this our tea boy burst into peals of laughter! I think the chap actually survived.

If you went out of the hanger toward the main gate, half way up the yard on the left was the dope shop, totally manned by women under a forewoman named Mabel. It was quite unsafe for any male to enter this shop, unless he was in a gang and even then it was very doubtful! Dope was used to stretch and waterproof one or two moveable pieces which were covered by fabric.

While I was in No 3 shop, the experiment of a 'piggy-back' aircraft was made. The object of this exercise was to get mail to Australia in one non-stop journey. For this a small seaplane, rather like the Schneider trophy aircraft was to be used, but as it had such a weight of fuel it could not lift off itself off the ground. The idea was for it to be taken up on the back of an Empire Flying Boat which, when high enough, would allow the 'riding aircraft' to break away and fly off on its own.

We usually got a tip-off when something like this was about to happen so a group of us would go outside and over the river to watch. I did a small job on Mercury, the seaplane but found it so cramped inside, I had to crawl around. Its engines were Napier and the cylinders were in the form on an "H" geared to three prop shafts. Mayo, the mother plane, was a standard Empire boat with a cradle and release mechanism positioned on top. A loud "crack" was emitted when the two aircraft parted.

The Stirling, built by Short Brothers was the first purpose built four engined bomber used in World War 11, but it turned out inferior to its rivals and by 1943 had been relegated to reconnaissance and other duties. One of our projects involved the construction of a half size version.

Another experimental job, not done at the Seaplane works but in the hangers on the airport, was constructing a half-sized version of the proposed Stirling bomber. Later I worked with the foreman –his name was Jimmy Carpenter, who became a works manager. He had literally built this plane in wood and fabric, to pencil sketches on envelopes. It had four Pobjoy 90hp engines – in 1934 Pobjoy moved its plant to Rochester to be near to Shorts but the ongoing effects of the Great Depression drove the company into liquidation, it was subsequently bought outright by Short Brothers.

This little plane was very fast and manoeuvrable and was later claimed to have been used as a basis for the De Havilland Mosquito, a twin-engine aircraft of plywood monocoque construction. After trials it was flown to Farnborough for Air Ministry checks and rumour has it that in the course of time, Short Bros. was duly telephoned and asked to please collect it. When the Test Pilot arrived to make the pick up, he was shown the aircraft in a thousand pieces, all laid out neatly!

We also built three Flying Boats for Imperial Airways which were just like the Empire boats but much larger, with about twice the passenger capacity. If I remember correctly the Empire only carried 24 passengers. The larger versions were named *The Golden Fleece* and *The Golden Hind.* When they were delivered to Southampton, it was reported they were having trouble with the tail plane controls while operating in the tropics. It was caused through the expansion of the hull and non-expansion of the steel controls, which kept cooler as they were inside. I forget what we did, but a gang of us went down to Southampton for a couple of weeks to work on them. I think the Flying Boats finally ended up in the Solent and were still there at the end of the war.

Whenever we went to Southampton as a gang we found somewhere to stay—all of us together. It was a clean place with just a dormitory where six of us slept. My bed was a bit damp the first night from which I suffered a little later. The breakfast was good and the price of two shillings and six pence (old money) per night and breakfast!

On the ferry over, I noticed a launch with staff going to Vosper Ltd (prior to 1936 it was Vosper & Co.) and among these, a pretty girl in a fur coat. She was not a beauty by any means, but attractive. Anyways I don't remember how I made contact, but it ended up with me, plus another chap, taking her out each night. It certainly relieved the boredom and we went to all the local theatres etc. We walked her home but she insisted at being left at the end of her road; it never went any further, think I was a bit naïve then – Shirley was her name, all we ever knew her by. I wonder if she survived the later bombing.

The long awaited and expected war was at last a fact, and on the Monday when we went into the works it was minus a lot of people, as many of them had signed on for the Territorial Army–good news really as the rest of us was put on extra hours. However within a week or so all the Terriers were back at the works. Apparently you can train anyone to become a soldier, but it takes many years to become a skilled craftsman! Building aircraft was rated as more important. For some time it became a phoney war as nothing much happened. Suddenly Dunkirk happened, and I saw many of the trains crossing Rochester Bridge with a very grimy and battered load upon load of soldiers.

About this time a notice went up on the board asking for suitable people to join the planning staff for 'Stirling production' at Rochester Airport. I immediately applied and was selected; my overalls were exchanged for a suit!

The planning office was run by a very nice Scotsman, Bob Grant, with all the degrees in engineering one could hope for, but rather too nice a character for a boss. However we all settled in and became a good team; our office was on the north side of the main hangar where the Stirling bombers were being assembled, about three or four in line, the main hangar doors just outside our office.

The phoney war was on at the time with very little happening. At this time we had a contractor come over painting the hanger roof. These painters found that it was great fun, when the air raid siren sounded, to slide down the ropes from the roof and run. Everyone else followed their example and ran too, emptying the works in no time. It was okay for the first few times but became monotonous after a while, although it was surprising how fast the buildings emptied.

One night a single German bomber came over and dropped a stick of bombs of which just one hit the boiler house. We didn't realise it at the time but this single aircraft must have been a pathfinder. About three days after this the siren went in the afternoon – a warm lazy September afternoon. The contractor boys did their stuff and the works emptied in double quick time.

I was sitting in the sun on a shelter top. By modern standards a pretty poor construction consisting of a small trench with a curved corrugated iron top and a couple of feet of earth overall with light modern doors; a gap at the top provided light while benches were arranged for seating inside. I was sitting on the top with another chap enjoying the afternoon sun and in the distance a small plane appeared. I remarked to my friend, "Oh, one of ours but perhaps we had better go inside in case". It was as well that we did as a few minutes after, all hell was let loose. One brave, or was it foolish, chap was looking out of the door top and gave us a running commentary on all that was going on – 'oxygen cylinders flying out of the roof, split like bananas' etc. As soon as the 'All Clear' sounded we trooped out to survey the damage and found holes everywhere. Even inside we found a finished Stirling split in two and the next in line had a large lump missing. Sinister unexploded bombs could be seen sticking out of the floor, but compared to modern bombing, and even later war bombing, these were quite small, probably around 250lbs. Of the two thousand men there were no fatalities, just a few wounds; we were really lucky. I noticed how the bomb splinters had pierced 1/2 inch steel with ease.

Now the job of clearing up started. The Ministry in their incredible wisdom put the roof back on, this time it was corrugated iron. Although we had plenty of shelters, we were told that if we wished we could leave the field and make for the wooded valley which ran on the north side of the airfield. The thing to do was to watch the gun emplacement manned by regulars, and when the canvas came off – and still more when the six Hurricanes from Gravesend flew over low – it was time to get ready to run.

The woods were near Fort Halsted where a naval six-inch gun was situated, and at times I could see the shells just after they had left the gun– this was in between dodging the shrapnel pattering through the trees. It's funny how one always felt that there was a safer place than the one you were in at the time! You have to resist the impulse to continually move.

The German air force gave us a couple of weeks or so to get the roof on again before proceeding to knock it off again. The 'powers that be' decided that there was little future in remaining at Rochester airfield so we were moved down to the seaplane works.

At the Seaplane works, the shelters were dug into the steep bank, there was almost a cliff behind the works itself and one could hear nothing. There were steel doors at the entrances, and when the bombers were close the call went out on the tannoy to "Close all tunnel doors." The only time damage was done was one night when a landmine dropped and rolled down the bank near the main gate which it demolished. I believe a housing estate now resides on the location of the old works.

For most of us in the planning office there was little to do at this time. The heads of departments had been sent to various locations, ours had gone to Stratton St Margaret, near Swindon in Wiltshire, to a large private house–they had apparently taken over "The Close". The Seaplane works was moved to an assembly plant near Windermere Lake.

I seemed to wait for weeks for the call to re-locate but nothing happened. In the end I packed my bags and, taking rather a gamble, climbed into my little Austin 7 Saloon and drove up to Swindon, where I located the office and went in to see my old boss Bob Grant. "Hello David, what are you doing here?" was his somewhat surprised greeting. I told him there was nothing doing at Rochester so I had decided to move. "Well, now you are here, you had better stay" he said, and stay I did.

It appeared that there was no schedule of all the parts that went into a Stirling bomber so I was detailed to deal with the wings. I was told to give a progress report to the top man, an efficiency expert, every week, which changed to fortnightly, then monthly before finally petering out altogether. It seemed to me that no-one really wanted this schedule at all. Being very bored and in a fit of pique one day I dropped all the files behind the row of filing cabinets and that was that!

During his time I had been detailed to do a secret job, which was quite interesting. We had shadow factories being erected around Swindon – wings at Sevenhampton, parts at Blunsdon, assembly at Flight Sheds near Stratton St Margaret and No 24 Shop G.W.R.(the old wagon repair sheds) a machine shop.

In order that the management in Head Office, still in Rochester, could see what progress was being made with the buildings, I was detailed to go round all the sites with a photographer, a Mr Maylott, who had a photographic business in Swindon. I had little plans on which I marked up the direction of each photograph. I always made a point of seeing each works manager to get permission before going on a site. This had a funny but very pleasant outcome. One works manager was Jimmy Carpenter, a man for whom I had the greatest respect, and who I came to like very much. He was of the real old craftsman class and had been in charge of the building of the half size Stirling which he had virtually done from sketches on the back of envelopes, as I mentioned earlier. Jimmy had liked the look of me, and one day he walked in to see my boss and in his blunt way said, "I want him as my assistant". And he got me!

I think I enjoyed my time working with him more than any other time during the war. I had what was the secretaries' office, next to his, and we shared the same secretary.

At this time tools, supplies of bits and pieces as well as sub-contractors were hard to get and one of my tasks was to scour the countryside for odds and ends. This was interesting work bringing me in touch with some real old characters.

There was a firm at Wantage that I visited from time to time, the first visit of which was memorable! The firm was Nalder & Nalder owned by two brothers. One of the pair was a rather fierce chap with a bristling moustache and county tweeds complete with deer stalker. "Are you from the Air Ministry?" he balled. "No sir, I'm from a private firm, Short Bros, aircraft builders." "Oh that's all right," he replied, "I was about to throw you out, bloody Air Ministry pinched some of my fields." So we got on well, most of my contacts from then on were with his manager, a quiet man but businesslike. The firm made machinery for the colonies, for coffee and tea plantations etc, lots of weir screw conveyers etc.

At Shorts' Sevenhampton factory we made wings for the Stirling, and Jimmy asked me if I could get some 10 ton lifting shackles, as they couldn't find any. These were "U" shackles, high tensile steel and made of about 3/8 inch or 1/2 inch round steel. So I trotted off to the G.W.R. works in Swindon and was directed to their chain department, the foreman showed me round his workshop and then the chain and coupling hook test equipment. The chains were tested in a covered channel in the floor, where they were stretched until they broke. "10 ton shackles? Of course we will make you some." In due course I had a phone call that our shackles were ready and I went off and collected them – the joke was that instead of nice neat little shackles of 3/8 material, these were terribly big, made of about 3/4 inch diameter steel – it caused a lot of laughter. They were never used! It seemed that '10 tons' differed between railway and aircraft. After some months, Jimmy was moved to the Blunsden factory and I went with him. Life went on much as usual as far as I can remember, at this factory we made fuselages which were fitted out at Sevenhampton, while wings and smaller parts were manufactured in Swindon Railway Works. These parts were taken to South Marston for assembly in a purpose-built factory.

At this time there was an acute shortage of skilled workmen and one day the manpower manager came round to see if he could raise any more skilled personnel. And the inevitable happened – finding I was a skilled man, I was told that I was more use to the war effort using my skill, and that someone without such skills could do my present job. So back on the tools I had to go, financially this was no loss and I managed to get away from shift work and work nights only.

I came in one night and found that the 8 ft guillotine on which we cut sheet steel was out of use due to a broken arm. This was a snag, so the only thing to do was repair it! Being a casting, this wasn't easy; furthermore I wasn't an expert welder, but 'nothing ventured', and it wasn't any use in its moribund condition. It took me the whole night, but by morning it was working again.

The next night I got the report! Jimmy had come in and his remark was, "There is only one person who could have done this – that bugger Curwen. God bless him."

I enjoyed my eighteen months of nights at Blunsdon, I had a very good friend who shared my bench, and as well as making a lot of press tools we managed to get in a little fun. In those days I had quite a collection of motor and motorcycle bits and among these was a motorcycle magneto. The drills we used were the usual Desoutter air drills and we made one of these to drive the magneto very slowly. We put a piece of thin wire onto the bench under a few pieces of metal, and anyone stopping for a chat invariably put a hand down to pick up the curious piece of metal only to receive a harmless surprise. I shared my bench with a Welshman, Jones by name, who came from Yeovil; he went back to Westland Works after the war.

The night work manager or foreman was a good friend especially as I had covered up a little 'fling' he was having with a very attractive night sister!

One night he came over and said "Come with me, very quietly, and bring your magneto. You might be able to help with a small problem I have and in which I do not want to take drastic action."

We entered the Sheet Metal Store and on tiptoe approached the central metal rack. The light alloy sheets were laid flat in the racks and there, fairly well hidden in the centre, and fast asleep, was the elderly storekeeper. We dangled a wire from a rod, fishing-rod fashion, so that it lightly touched his nose, and wound the magneto – the reaction was immediate – he bumped his head on the sheets above it, and in the general confusion we silently withdrew. We believe it had the desired effect.

My friend and bench mate Jones, I forget his first name, and I used to take our midnight sandwiches to the boiler house in the winter. It was the warmest place, and the boiler-man was a particularly good chap. Every now and again we'd fall asleep and if we had overrun our break time he either woke us up, or if he thought we were looking tired, covered us up with sacks for and let us sleep on.

One night one of the gauge glasses broke, like a gunshot, and filled the house with steam before he could close the cocks, this is the only time in my life experience of steam that a glass has blown near me. Steam is a good servant … The Blunsdon factory was situated deep in the countryside and well I recall the song of the crickets, there were dozens of them taking refuge in the warm boiler-house.

By 1941 I had moved to Gore Lane Farm at Baydon. Night work was sometimes quite tiring and there were times when, on my early morning six mile return trip to Baydon, things became a little scary. I had a Ford 10 saloon, which I had bought cheaply from one of the storekeepers, and on one occasion during a dark winter morning I was returning home with my usual passenger who lodged in Baydon. Suddenly he shouted "Mind!" and I saw in the glimmer of my blacked headlamps, a cycle rear light near my right-hand side. I made a violent swerve and missed him; I could tell by the very wobbly cycle light caught in my rear-view mirror.

On another occasion I was speeding home when a sudden jolt woke me up, and I found I was careering along the right hand bank which sloped away from the road at an angle of nearly 45 degrees. Fortunately I had enough sense to accelerate hard and pull the car back onto the road.

What was nearly the end of the Ford came on another early morning, I was trundling along on a straight level stretch when suddenly there was an almighty bang, a shower of sparks by my feet and the car did a hefty leap before coming to a rapid halt. Silence! Looking in the mirror I could see oil and metal behind me in the road. On lifting the bonnet I could see a con rod sticking out from the side of the engine.

How I got the car home I do not remember, but in the end I managed to buy another engine and get it once more into action. In those days it was a quick and easy task to swap over an engine, unlike today!

The Stirling bomber was losing its usefulness as its ceiling height was only sixteen thousand feet, well in range of the Germans fighters. Avro and others were taking over. Once again I found myself marking time; I cannot clearly remember just the sequence of events. I had a short period in the offices at Plesseys in Kembury Street, Swindon, but eventually I was transferred to Vickers, South Marston, for a spell in the planning office on Spitfire development. It was, without doubt the unhappiest job I had experienced so far. For eighteen months I had little to do, and amused myself by making a friend of the machine shop foreman to whom I would talk when I got too bored. To make things worse we had to do two nights of overtime for nothing! And there were thirty five of us in this office.

Being really fed up at Vickers I applied for a job with Dowty Engineering and went to the Cheltenham office for an interview. To my surprise I got the job which was to be the supply chaser in Coventry, but when I applied for my release, Vickers would not give it! So I went to see the Manpower Board representative, who I had met before at Short Brothers, and asked if he could do anything about it? He said that if Vickers said no, there was nothing he could do about it, so that was that. I think Vickers was on a wonderful contract basis with the Government, "Cost Plus", so they got 10% on my wages, and the more they had on the staff, the higher their profit! In the time of war, this wasn't a nice way to do business as it seemed to be taking advantage and was dishonest.

At this time, the war with Germany was drawing to a close, and it was not worth the risk of the sack by punching someone on the nose, and ending up in the army of occupation for some years. So the only thing to do was to stick it out for the time being at any rate. As it happened this wasn't long as the German wars came to an end with the Japanese war following suit. I could now obtain my release—and noted that anyone wanting to engage in some kind of peacetime work project was being encouraged.

I remember an interesting conversation I had with one of our planning staff at Vickers before I left. He was an ex-Merchant Navy man of early middle age, who said "You know, I fear for this country; we are getting too politically-minded, I have travelled the world many times before this war, and noticed that in any country in which politics started to take over, it just spelled disaster in the end." True, how very true, I have now reached the age of 94, and, looking back, I have seen politicians give away our Empire, which kept half the world in peace! If it did nothing else! It developed countries, only to give them up to disastrous self-rule. We were manufacturers to the world – coal, steel, shipbuilding, motor cars and motor cycles and all this has gone, and as a last resort they are talking about giving away our Sovereignty.

Chapter 5

Our first business venture

While I was at the Blunsdon factory I had become friendly with Richard Ripley, one of the other workers. He was a well-educated man who had his own small printing firm in South West London. He had expressed a wish to join me if I ever started a small engineering business of my own, so now seemed a good time to put this plan into action. So in 1946 I acquired a small overdraft from the bank and obtained the use of the corn store in the farm barn near my house on the Russley Park Estate. It was a good building wood lined throughout, with a huge water tank in the roof, which supplied both house and farm; it must have contained several thousand gallons. In a field there was a wooden shed with a Lister D type hopper-cooled stationary engine driving a Climax pump, which we ran fortnightly to fill the tank.

Several times during our tenancy the pump rods broke and a well-known firm of Water Engineers, Whatley of Pewsey, would come out and repair it. Judging by the number of rods it must have been a very deep bore hole. The rod breakage is a thing I have come across before; they seem to crystallize with age, due possibly to the cold they are always subject to.

It has to be said that the loft was not a very suitable place from which to run an engineering business, but Richard Ripley joined me there, and via an advert or two in the *Model Engineer* we obtained a little work. I installed my 3½ inch flat bed Drummond lathe, and also moved our engine driven lighting plant up there as well. In referring to the lighting plant, there is of course a tale to tell. When I first came to Wiltshire houses were very hard to come by, but we had a good Welfare Officer, a Mrs McNully, and after hunting high and low she came to me one day and said, "I have found a remote farmhouse in the country, are you interested?" She took me into the wilds of Wiltshire, way up onto the downs, where I was confronted by two cottages, at Gore Lane Farm, which had been made into one house–which I immediately fell for. My landlord was Sonny Hall, a trainer living at Russley Park, Baydon, and the farm belonged to him. There was one toilet plus a cold water tap, supplied from the barn I have just referred to.

Water was supplied to the farm at Russley Park by a Lister D type driving a Climax pump—rather like this one. It was housed in a wooden shed and ran fortnightly to fill a vast water tank.

There was also no electric light – Russley Park had its own generator – and no sewage. On my journey back to arrange for furniture removal etc I called at a scrap dealer I knew at Kingsdown on the main Maidstone-London road, near Brands Hatch, and bought a 50 volt Austinlite Automatic plant for £10. Then I arranged for the furniture van to pick it up on route.

This little plant is worth describing. It was all-in-one, a casting forming the base incorporating the single cylinder engine and the generator, the engine was 4-stroke petrol and there was a small electric control box which cut the engine in, using the generator or dynamo to turn it, all arranged that when the batteries started to get low the engine would start and stop when they were charged.

As there were no batteries, I managed to get four second-hand car batteries, and in a week, wired the house and got it running.

The method of choking for starting from cold was very ingenious indeed. The carburettor was without a float chamber and was formed with a small chamber about 2 inch diameter by 1½ inches deep, with an elbow suction pipe to the engine on top, and a pipe about ¾ inch by 4 inches long beneath. The petrol was fed in the bottom of this and the jet was about level with the bottom of the 2 inch chamber. The petrol tank was very shallow and was so arranged that when full it had to be of such a height that the petrol was nearly level with the jet. The 2 inch bottom of the chamber had a ring of small holes about ¼ inch diameter and each hole had a ball bearing in it, and through these holes the air flowed when the engine was running; but on starting the ball sealed the chamber and thus gave the engine a very rich

When we moved the workshop from the corn store to the chicken-house we bought another Austin lighting plant, this time a twin-cylinder 100 volt version complete with batteries. It was essential to have more power to drive line-shafting and power tools. Sadly the Austin was coming to the end of its working life as the water passages were starting to fur up causing the castings to crack. We subsequently replaced it with a modern 10hp Ruston & Hornsby which was much more capable of tackling the job required.

mixture, being kept off their seats by the airflow when the engine was running.

The only major trouble that I had with this plant was failure of the field coils in the generator and dynamo. At the time, wire of this style was difficult to obtain, but I happened to know an electrician in Swindon who managed to locate some. I had to set about re-winding the field coils myself but, at the same time thanking my lucky stars it wasn't the armature, as re-winding that would have foxed me completely. At the time I recall having a large carbuncle on the back of one hand. One day, while swinging this Austin, it decided to kick back and the handle struck my hand so hard that it completely swiped off the carbuncle, which was useful as I was thinking of having it surgically removed!

So with the power plant up and running, plus the use of an old Burnerd lathe, we were in a position to tackle some of the work that came in via the advert in the *Model Engineer*. There was also an interest in the possibility of doing something with steam cars. Two chaps named Bower and Bell had designed a steam pump which could be made on a small lathe, the engine was a compound and quite small as it was designed to work at 1500 lbs per square inch. If my memory is correct it had a high pressure cylinder of 1¹/4 inches diameter, the low being 2¹/4 inches with a short stroke.

We finally fitted the engine in an MG car using a coal fired flash boiler which the owners had bought from the Bolsover Brothers, who had been experimenting for some time on steam road vehicles.

It was not a success. We had a terrible time getting steam out of the flash boiler and once when we did, the safety valve lifted at 1200 lbs per square inch – the outlet was piped to the ground and it blew a hole 12 inches by 8 inches deep! At the time I had a young black Labrador dog and it just happened to be leaning against the front wheel when the steam exploded out. Needles to say he disappeared in a cloud of dust but didn't return home for about six hours!

The subject of steam cars is an interesting one and well worth a complete chapter in order to detail certain reminiscences.

Chapter 6

Steam cars and other troubles

Just after the war there was a renewed interest in steam vehicles. Some of this was no doubt due to the difficulty of getting petrol, but apart from this there was a definite interest in the subject and many experiments were carried out.

It might be a good idea to give a very brief history of the cars to this time. In the early days of automobile travel, the steam car and the internal combustion engine driven car were rivals, and if anything the steam car was on top. The Stanley car from America was for years the best method of reliable transport. The firm, founded by the two Stanley brothers, made a lot of cars. In 1906 Fred Marriott set a land speed record of 127.66 mph in a Stanley steam powered car called The Rocket, a record which remained unbroken for many years. When the car crashed into the sea during a later attempt Stanley Brothers forbade further attempts!

There were basically two different types of car. The Stanley, and several later makes, had a boiler for steam generation; basically a vessel with a capacity of water in it. The Stanley boiler in the 10 hp car was a vertical cylinder of 18 inches diameter with fire tubes fired by paraffin. There were later water tube boilers by other makers, but all had a quantity of water in them.

The other types, the American White, the French Serpollet and finally the Doble, had what can be described as steam generators, rather than boilers, they had grids or coils of tube which were heated and water pumped through them which instantly flashed into steam. These were called flash steam (or mono-tube) generators as they were in fact one length of tube, preferably with thick walls, your reserve was not a lot of hot water, as per Stanley, it was heat retained in the walls of the tube, and this was a very much smaller reserve, and the Doble had a very complicated control system, difficult then but easier now, both the pumps supplying the water and the burner supplying the heat were electrically controlled and had to be co-ordinated.

The steam car engine was direct coupled to the car rear axle, no method of clutching or free running, and the water pump was driven by the engine. So if you were low on steam on a hill and needed water, you were, not to put too fine a point on it, stymied!

Providing the Stanley, or water-tube boiler, was kept reasonably full you had capacity for some time. Controls were simple, with a thermostat keeping water up to a pressure to control the oil fire, so it all worked well.

The mono-tube on a flash generator is perfectly safe – a burst tube means an instant loss of pressure, a hiss, a cloud of steam, but no explosion. A boiler with a quantity of water is lethal. You are trapping a lot of water at very high temperature and pressure, a fracture releases the pressure instantly, the whole quantity of waters burst into steam with devastating results.

Having said that, I never heard of a Stanley boiler bursting, but as a bit of a safety measure, the barrel was bound tightly with a huge quantity of piano wire.

We made several steam car engines to order, one a poppet valve 4-cylinder radial, quite a good simple design. Sadly I never heard how well that one went as it was supplied to a hopeful builder–as we know many projects were never finished.

We were approached by a country doctor from Oxfordshire who had somehow acquired the steam car bug, and thought he might become rich and famous if he could put together a car and possibly put it on the market. He certainly had grand ideas.

A chap named Harman Lewis was acting as a consultant for us, he was an engineer with a Doble that he'd done much work on. He told us of a man in Sheffield who had very nearly completed a steam car conversion on the Doble principle, but owing to health and business commitments could go no further and wished to sell it. So I put it to the doctor and he bought it.

The next thing was to get it from Sheffield to our Wiltshire based works in Baydon. "Oh, tow it down," said the doctor. I asked him if he had ever been towed, to which he replied no, but was game to have a go– he'd been to sea in a trawler and was game for anything! I can't quite see how this made him a suitable chap for towing as he was a bit of a nervous type, but anyhow that's how it was left.

The day finally arrived, and we set off for Sheffield, where we arrived just after lunch, but by the time everything was stowed, the bills paid and the car on tow (it was a heavy old Morris saloon, one of their largest), it was 4 pm getting dusk, and raining hard. So off we went, and hadn't gone very far when there were shouts from the Doc – "Not so fast, not so fast!" – he was getting a little fraught. Anyhow, I slowed down, and the miles ticked by. After some 75 miles of tedious towing, petrol was getting low so I drew in at some pumps, filled up, and asked the bloke how far we were from our destination near Oxford? He answered, "Never 'eard of it." I tried somewhere else – same answer. Getting a little fed up with this I asked," Well, how far are we from Sheffield then?" "Oh, fifteen miles about, just up the road ..." We, or rather I, had taken a wrong turn somewhere and we had driven a complete circle!

We drove on to Chesterfield and put up at an hotel for

the night. The doctor was a bit peeved, and I was fed up as it was really my fault for agreeing to do the trip with him. He just wasn't the type for a task of this nature.

We got the car to our works the next day and over the next few months did a lot of work on it. Quite frankly, it was a pain in the neck. The Stanley 20 engine was quite wrong for a car of this sort with a Doble type, high pressure 1,000-1,500 lb sq ins. high superheat, steam generator – the Stanley worked at about 650 lbs and not very hot steam.

When we finally got it going, each time we went for a test run something always failed within a mile. A con rod broke and pushed a piston out of the top of the cylinder, the hot steam wore the slide valves completely out so a complicated piston valve conversion designed by Harman Lewis was duly installed. We had trouble with the burner – 12 volt motors were not so good in 1948 – but finally it did drive okay. I delivered it to the doctor who lived near Didcot, a trip of about thirty miles. It went quite well, and I showed him how to work it, but I doubt he ever ventured out in it.

What actually happened to the car I am not sure, but some years later I read a series of articles by a chap who was telling readers about the wonderful things he was doing, re-designing and building a car he had bought, and by the description this was the same vehicle.

Harman Lewis came down several times in his Doble, all the way from Ewell or Esher, I forget which. It went okay but had one terrible fault; it was always difficult to keep the batteries up. The engine of these cars was direct on the back axle with about a 2-1 gearing. So there wasn't any really fast shaft from which to run a dynamo, and alternators were not in use yet, so if your battery tended to be a bit low, it did not run the burner fan fast enough. The result being incomplete combustion of paraffin which doesn't half make your eyes water! I can never understand why they had not tried to duct the exhaust away as the boiler or generator fired from the top so burnt fumes came out at the bottom right under your feet, and permeated upwards through the floor boards.

A chap named Taylor (from Bristol) had an old Stanley 10 hp that he had rebuilt, and he came over in it and gave me a ride. It was not sophisticated like the Doble. In this car, of about 1910 vintage, you sat out in the open, but even so it was charming, dead quiet, very smooth and altogether a lovely. My father-in-law had one of these when he was the M.D of the Vulcan Foundry; he used it to fetch the midwife when my wife was about to be born although she arrived in this world before the Stanley returned!

Before we go over to railway locomotives I would like to break chronological order to tell you of the last steam car I became involved with. When I returned from working at the Talyllyn Railway (described later), we had bought a millwright-cum-agricultural business in Devizes. It had a very large blacksmith's drill with a drill table about 3ft diameter. I should say that my original partner had by this time left and been replaced by Edgar Newbery, who I have described later in Chapter 9.

One day, after a little correspondence, two city type gents came to see us as they had heard of my steam car experiences. They asked I could make them a Doble type flash boiler to which, being a glutton for punishment, I agreed.

They sent down all the tube required and my father-in-law and I started to make the pancake coils. We did this by using the large circular plate of the drill and with 1/4 inch thick spacers wound the coils by fixing the tube to a centre spigot and turning the table with a bar. A task easier than it sounds here! Finally came the welding of spacers to keep the tubes (now in the form of a clock spring) in place with enough gaps.

From time to time the two aforementioned chaps came down for a progress report and always took me out to lunch. Curiosity got the better of me one day and I asked if it was to be a private venture? The younger of the two surreptitiously whispered to his friend, "Can we tell him?" The answer was yes provided I kept it very strictly secret. The elder man was Singer Motor Company's chief designer, the other his assistant, and they were thinking of producing a special steam car for enthusiasts.

After this I was taken fully into their confidence. I found a Sentinel 4-cylinder single acting lorry engine for them to dismantle and study, from which they designed a 4-cylinder single acting engine and had converted a Singer back axle to 2-1 gearing. Finally they asked if I would, in strict secrecy, complete the chassis to a runner.

We had one very good fitter, George Bevan, who we installed in an old storeroom behind locked doors. In the course of time everything was together, and we could raise steam to a working pressure of 1,500 lbs per sq in 90 seconds. We tried it enthusiastically up and down the yard. One day just as we were doing this my new business partner Edgar Newbery arrived. As he was a steam enthusiast he begged for a ride, so we installed him on a cushion on the rear member before George opened the throttle. Well, when you open 1,500 lbs to an engine, it certainly provides quite a punch. Poor old Mr Newbury, and his cushion, were shot onto the floor!

During the time I was working for Singer, several visits to Coventry were made. On one of these, the Chief Designer said, "Our Chairman would like to see you." So along we went and I was quietly ushered into a panelled office, with the ancestors' portraits on the walls. The Chairman was a white-haired noble figure who addressed me in a hushed voice, "I understand you are helping us with this project, Mr Curwen?" "Yes sir, that is so, I replied". "Good, good, I am sure you will do your best for us, we thank you. Goodbye." I was ushered out even quicker than my entry, talk about short and sweet!

They came and collected the chassis, placing it under a sheet on an unmarked lorry, and some weeks after said everything was going well. I believe they had started on what would be the second one. Then Rootes took the firm over, and after a time I wrote to Mr, or rather Lord Rootes, to see if I could be of any further help? I was told the project had been dropped. A great pity as it had a chance for success.

These steam cars were just a small part of our early days as Richard Ripley and I had really started off with the intention of selling our model locomotives that we advertised in the *Model Engineer*. Let's take a closer look at that side of the business.

Chapter 7

Farmyard Engineering!

A little spasmodic work came in and then we got the chance of moving from our corn loft to a disused chicken house of the large style, probably the forerunner of a battery type—large sheds for 20,000 or more hens. It was a good building with plenty of light, all one side being glass. We started to turn this into a workshop by installing a line shaft to drive machines, and managed to buy from a farmer friend a twin cylinder Austin-lite 100 volt lighting plant complete with batteries. By this time War Surplus equipment was being sold and we obtained a hefty 6 inch or 8 inch lathe – I cannot remember the make – and a good shaper, plus various other tools, and these were all driven by the twin-cylinder Austin lighting plant until a spate of troubles struck. The Austin engine had rather small water passages, and over the years these had become furred up and cracks started to appear, sadly it had reached the end of its working life.

1948 David Curwen Limited ***Miniature Locomotives*** *catalogue lists the following ex-works prices. Atlantic Type 4-4-2 £1,250, Pacific Type 4-6-2 £1,500 with £100 extra for a copper boiler! Our standard gauge was 10 1/4 inch which we found quite adequate for all practical purposes. These locomotives will pull loads from 50 to 100 passengers.*

We had met a very helpful machinery dealer named Bond, at a surplus auction near Ramsbury and he had quite a few stationary engines for sale, so we visited his store which I think was down in the Westbury area. Here we found a 10 hp open crank Ruston & Hornsby paraffin engine which was almost new, having been a standby set and hardly used. I cannot remember what it cost but probably between £10 and £20 but it proved its weight in gold.

The only near mishap occurred one day when the 3 inch wide leather belt, driving the shafting, broke and somehow caught in the crankshaft and started flailing around in a devilish manner. In order to dodge the swishing belt and reach the paraffin tap on the tank by the wall, I had to keep well back and then make a lunge. The whole operation was fraught with danger but somehow I managed it, but it was a 'near miss' and clearly illustrates how unexpected dangers are always lurking around the corner.

We managed to get quite a variety of work and finally had about six chaps working for us. Mr Newbury had nearly finished a 7 1/4 inch gauge Immingham 4-6-0 so we completed this and it was sold to a chap in Herne Bay. I recall his name was Mr Liversedge; he was a very good craftsman and built quite a few locos in the larger gauges. His only fault lay in his boiler-making, always using too thin material; I remember he showed us a copper boiler for a 5 inch gauge loco, which had bulged between all the barrel joints. When he asked what I thought of it I had to be tactful by saying that possibly it would have been better with rather thicker sheets!

Funnily enough, some years ago I was asked to re-boiler a King class G.W.R. locomotive in 7 1/4 inch gauge for Robin Lee-Pemberton's brother. The locomotive ran on their Torrey Canyon Railway. The workmanship of the four-cylinder loco was first class, very good, but once again the steel boiler was made of far too thin a gauge of plate. I forget what had actually failed in the old boiler but we were told they wanted it returned– to one of the sons. Apparently father had told son that if he wanted to buy something, maybe a car or a motor-cycle, he could sell all the scrap round the estate and farm to raise the money. So that was why the old boiler was required. A pity many other fathers did not do likewise with their sons! This one was a good tactician!

Back to 1948 - I forget how I came in contact with Bassett-Lowke, but we started to do a little work for them. This was probably because the war had sadly reduced the number of skilled men they employed. Bassett-Lowke had a contract for making demonstration models of Bailey bridges, to teach the troops how to assemble them, but with the cessation of hostilities this contract had run its course.

We built them a 3½ inch gauge 0-6-0 tank engine, and had a firm of draughtsmen from Newbury to detail it out; the object being to sell it as a kit comprising castings with drawings for the DIY enthusiast. When we had finished the loco, we took it to their London showroom where the manager Herbert Sell had intended to paint it. But having seen it, Mr Sell thought it so good in brass that he put it on show where it remained for many years. The chap who made this engine for us was an ex-Swindon bus driver who gave up his job due to stomach ulcers. He turned out to be a natural craftsman and a great asset to our firm.

On one of my many trips to Bassett-Lowke at Northampton, I met Mr B-L himself but the great man was far too grand to do more than pass the time of day with lesser mortals like myself. However his co-director Mr Franklin, who managed the firm's finances, was an entirely different matter and took me to his house and showed me his own 9½ inch gauge railway. After the deaths of these two, I dealt with H.W.Franklin (son of H.F.R. Franklin, Bassett-Lowke's joint founder) and Roland Fuller, who ran the firm from then on. Both became good friends who did many favours for us over the years.

We had six employees at the time, among who was an elderly model– maker who used to come in at weekends to fiddle about with various ongoing projects. He was a dear old bachelor who brought along his small treadle lathe with which to occupy his time. He perfected a small paraffin burner of which Bassett-Lowke bought a dozen or so to put in their catalogue under the old chap's name – 'The Pomeroy'.

Then we had our first real break, we had a visit from a wartime Naval petty officer, the son of a furniture removal firm in Reading. He could not settle down to business in an office. After years at sea he had, with a partner had laid a 10¼ inch railway at Hilsea Lido, which was the start of a park inland from Portsmouth just under the downs. He was using a hired loco which had been made by Bullock some years before and had seen better days; in fact it was a constant source of trouble.

He asked us if we could build him a loco that would do the job, and being the eternal optimist I immediately agreed, even though I had never built a loco of such considerable size before. Firstly we went down to Hilsea and had a look at the present Bullock locomotive. My impression was that mechanically it was rather too light. This was the moment that I decided that for miniature narrow gauge passenger locos built for pleasure parks and the like, one must forget the model which generally was a scaled down copy of a full size railway locomotive. It is essential to design something strong enough to tackle the job in hand, while at the same time making it look pleasing to the eye. My theory has been proved correct during my fifty years in locomotive manufacture. He wanted a Pacific and we finally settled on an L.N.E.R. A1, well to be politically correct an A2/1! At that time L.B.S.C. "Curly" the well-known writer in *Model Engineer* magazine had described a loco of this type, calling it *Highland Lassie*. I must say the design of the locomotive was extremely thorough, well thought out and, for us, a really interesting project.

In conjunction with a farmer landowner friend we decided we would build an extra locomotive for ourselves and put it through various tests, assuming of course we could find a site from which to use it.

Construction of the boiler was of course beyond us being rather heavy work, it was far better to give it to a professional boilermaker. At that time Tom Goodhand being a specialist in this field, was making boilers of exactly the type required. So I arranged a visit to Gillingham in Kent where I made the acquaintance of the dear old man who was tackling this type of work. He had a rambling old workshop, tucked up a very narrow lane. His glasses were so spattered and scratched from welding and grinding it was a wonder he could see at all. We discussed the job, "Do you want a detail drawing?" "No, no," said he, "we will just make a sketch of the outside sizes you want, I'll do the rest", and he did. As material was so hard to get, he said I had to find the 5/16 inch plate required for the task. I was lucky in having very good contacts so I picked it up the steel plate without much difficulty, the only downside was picking up a speeding ticket, for doing over 50 mph with a trailer, while delivering it to him! Speeding was just as much of a sin in those days.

We collected the boilers when they were ready, paying the reasonable sum of £100 each–those were the days!

My farmer friend, Stephen Brown who lived at Chieveley near Newbury, and I set about trying to find a suitable site for a railway, and Weymouth council was approached. We made an appointment to meet them. It was midwinter and Stephen suggested driving, it was freezing hard and the heater in his Ford 10 was pathetic to say the least. We had an afternoon meeting and found the Council to be quite amenable. We left in the early evening darkness, a cold drizzle and the odd wet snowflake, but as we drove further north into Wiltshire we found it to be snowing pretty hard. Stephen was a good driver who simply charged through the snow-drifts over Salisbury Plain but by the time we got to Aldbourne he said it would be nigh on impossible to climb the hill up to Baydon so could I possibly manage to walk the rest of the way? It was getting late so there was nothing for it. When I think back, I must have been pretty fit. It was difficult to see the hedges between one and two feet of snow but somehow I struggled up to Baydon and on down into the valley near Russley Park. The walk must have been a good three miles so it was such a relief to get home. I was wearing a heavy full length overcoat which was frozen stiff when I took it off; in fact it stood up by itself! Of course there was no central heating in those days and cooking was by Calor gas—we often had to warm the cylinders to get the gas to flow!

Anyhow the locos were finally finished by the spring in 1947 and the Hilsea engine was delivered. I invited Edgar Westbury and J.N. Maskelyne of *Model Engineer* magazine to come and see it. Admittedly they were very friendly and gave us a good write-up, but I always felt that it was not quite to their rather critical liking. It was built heavier, the wheel rims were larger than scale, it had Baker valve gear whereas the A1 L.N.E.R. had Walchearts, in other words it hadn't the right number of rivets and would not therefore win a prize! However it was a good design looked good and did its job. Both locomotives are still around today, one apparently lying around in storage while the other is undergoing a massive restoration by Joe Nemeth Engineering at Severn Beach. In October 2006, thanks to David Edgington, I was lucky enough to be re-united with this engine, which for a considerable number of years, has carried the name *Robin Hood*; when I originally built it I merely used a date numbering system--2647. Back in 1947 I never dreamt this locomotive would still be around some 60 years later, especially after such an extremely hard life, firstly at the Weymouth Miniature Railway, and then moving to Oakhill Manor. At one stage in its life it was even used at the Audley End Railway. The extensive rebuild by Joe Nemeth includes new axle boxes, a cylinder rebore and new pistons. I wonder if *Robin Hood* will still be around in another 60 years?

In reading an article in a magazine quite recently I find that I was not the first to get this idea of these locos being a machine in their own right. Twining, who was associated with Bassett-Lowke, had exactly the same idea, but was restricted a little by the B-L hierarchy, however he did build some locomotives on his own to his standard. One of these being *Sian*, which for many years ran on the Fairbourne Railway in Wales. Unfortunately a few years ago

2647 ***Robin Hood*** *arriving at Joe Nemeth Engineering in January 2005 after an extremely arduous life, ending its days working at Oakhill Manor railway. Photo by Joe Nemeth.*

In October 2006 I had the privilege of being re-united with 2647 ***Robin Hood*** *and comparing notes with engineer/restorer Joe Nemeth--seen here in the blue overalls while I look on. The quality of engineering, plus a modicum of loving care, being put into the rebuild of this locomotive should ensure another 60 years of providing pleasure at public events.*

this railway was sold, and the new owners altered the gauge and sold off the 15 inch locos, but I believe at least one has been saved and restored.

After building the two Pacific locomotives we picked up an order for two more from a Mr Briggs of Worthing. As I had come to the conclusion the Pacific would be a little heavy for small pleasure parks where curves in the track had to be fairly sharp, I devised a plan to leave out one pair of driving wheels making them Atlantics. In this configuration they did not conform to any British prototype so it seemed a good idea to Americanise them. Altogether we made five to this design plus a further one, made in the 1960's in my Devizes works, for Lowestoft. They became known as the Curwen Atlantics. Two went to Mr Briggs, two we kept and found a site at the Kursall in Southend, and one was an exported to Durban, South Africa.

When the Worthing site closed due to a disagreement with the council, the two engines were put into storage until, after a lengthy period, being purchased by Lord Gretton of Stapleford Park near Melton Mowbray. He was the first stately home to have a railway after the war.

He went to see the manager of Bassett-Lowke in High Holborn and asked if he should buy the two locos? When Herbert Sell asked Lord Gretton who made them? The latter answered, "Someone called Curwen". "Buy them," was the answer! One is still at Stapleford but I've sadly lost touch with the other one.

One of the Kursall (Southend) locos was bought by Robin Neville, now Lord Braybrooke. It ran for many years in its original form, but due to a pretty steep gradient, I decided to transform it into a 2-6-2 with a new boiler. Latterly a rebuild by Tony Crowhurst put the locomotive in fine order and she is still running, the cylinders have never been re-bored.

Chapter 8

Talyllyn Adventure

Some time in 1949 Roland Fuller of Bassett-Lowke asked if I would meet someone who was interested in refurbishing a narrow-gauge railway in Wales. In due course Tom Rolt (L.T.C.Rolt who later became the well-known author) came to see me. He was interested in the Talyllyn Railway in Wales, but as everything there was in a very dilapidated state, it was thought it might be a good idea to convert it to a 15 inch gauge line, like the Romney Hythe or the Ravenglass and Eskdale, so would I go up with him and take a cursory look? So it was arranged that we should go up to Wales and in due course I went to Stanley Pontlarge, a village near Cheltenham, where Tom lived in his parents' lovely old Cotswold house, with the G.W.R. in a cutting below the garden.

We embarked on the journey in Tom's very much vintage 1924 Alvis duck back tourer, a car which Tom drove with great skill. It was a good and reliable sports car, but it certainly wasn't warm inside as there were no heaters in those days. It was winter and despite rugs and an overcoat I can still remember how very cold I became as we drove over the passes into the mountains of Wales. The floor board of the Alvis did not entirely stop the wind!

We arrived at Towyn at dusk and Tom took me to the engine shed, where two men were trying to repair the frames of old *"Dolgoch"* (the railway's second locomotive) by very dim lighting, candles I think, or maybe an oil lamp. The track was in the last stages of decay and only one rather tired locomotive remained in service–at times when it failed, a 'NO TRAIN TODAY' notice was posted on the station gate at Towyn. We had a cursory look and then Tom took us to the Tynyconnel Hotel, a farmhouse on the shore of Talyllyn Lake, recently opened as a hotel. There was, of course, no central heating and hams hung from the ceilings, but even so the food and drink were good, the rooms clean, but no mod cons– I was very glad I had brought a hot water bottle in my bag.

One of the days of our stay was a Sunday, and after an evening meal the following amusing incident occurred. There was a knock on the door, Captain Hunter (the owner) answered it, and a male Welsh voice said, "Hey Captain Hunter, please could I have a drink?" To which the good Captain replied, "I'm very sorry but it's Sunday so I can't oblige you". "Oh Captain Hunter, Jones the Police said you could give me one". He was immediately given his drink.

We walked the railway, discussing it all the way, returned, and I think I gave him some rough figures of the cost of 15-inch gauge materials. We followed up with various meetings in Birmingham and Banbury with other like-minded people who had formed a committee with the idea of saving the railway. One of these enthusiasts was a Mr Trinder, and another Mr Russell. There were endless meetings with discussions and proposals of various schemes, as the Talyllyn's present owner, Sir Haydn Jones, wanted the railway to continue. After his death, as far as I was concerned, things went quiet but some time later Tom contacted me again saying a decision had been made to retain the railway by trying to revive it.

I had recently married Barbara Willans, not knowing at the time that Tom Rolt was now a cousin by marriage, this came as a surprise to us all, and through it we formed a lasting friendship. I have made mention of the marriage side of things just to show that engineers are not all dirt, oil, steel, nuts, bolts and spanners–there is another side to us! I'll just tell you how I came to meet my wife. Before doing so I should say, for the benefit of younger readers, that the Willans family were well known steam engineers, with Peter Willans—a brilliantly inventive mechanical engineer—being credited with inventing the central valve steam engine. These engines were developed in conjunction with Colonel R.E.B.Crompton, for electricity generation. Kyrle Willans, who I am about to mention, is Peter Willans' son.

Whilst I was at Baydon, Kyrle Willans got in touch with me, to see if I could manufacture some paddle wheels for a venture he had with Lord Sidmouth, involving turning ex-army landing craft into houseboats for use on the Kennet and Avon Canal. The Canal was so weed infested that a screw was out of the question. On one of his visits he brought his daughter with him; she was on the stage, but at this time 'resting'–I believe the term is, being between jobs. We passed the time of day, and it occurred to me that a little more investigating might not come amiss, so when the paddles were made, it was agreed that I deliver them. I duly telephoned only to find Mr Willans was out but his daughter said he'd left a message saying the paddles should be delivered to Baker's Garage at Woodborough.

Never to miss an opportunity I said, in all innocence of course, I wasn't quite sure where Baker's Garage was, so if I came and picked her up could she show me? Baker's Garage, indeed, I'd been there many times, maybe God will forgive me after 56 years of marriage!!

However, back to the Talyllyn Railway story. By 1951, a

voluntary society, comprising enthusiasts young and old, had been put together in an attempt to put the railway back into service as a viable proposition. Tom Rolt, who was General Manager for the first two years, asked if I would go up as Chief Mechanical Engineer when the society took over. I agreed and in due course we both set out for Towyn, from here the subsequent adventure is well documented in Tom Rolt's book *Railway Adventure*. The first year involved a real struggle just to keep the railway operating and although Tom's book covers the story in some depth I have a few amusing incidents worth recalling.

Initially Tom and I found some temporary accommodation in the village of Rhydyronen which was up the valley from Towyn. As far as accommodation goes, ours was quite reasonable. The toilet was situated outside over a stream. The bad side of this was the extreme cold when sitting out there in the winter but the good side, from a natural history point of view, was looking down watching all the little fish swimming in the water below.

This was when John Snell joined us. He was one of the Talyllyn Railway's first volunteer workers. He wrote to offer his services, in 1950, while a pupil at Bryanston School. In between leaving school and going to Oxford, and later during lengthy holidays, he was a keen and pragmatic member of the team. I taught him to drive the Talyllyn locomotive and he became the first driver of the society. When Barbara joined us, she became surrogate mother, mending his socks and tending him when he was down with flu. He later worked for London Transport but his last job was with the Romney Hythe and Dymchurch Railway.

Another memory of that hotel was one night when Barbara and I were nearly pitched onto the floor when one leg of the bed went through the floor.

In due course we moved to the Dolgoch Hotel run by Mrs Spratley Jones. Here we enjoyed good rooms in the hotel out of season, moving to inferior rooms when the season started! Barbara and I moved to an outside room above the wash- house, with stone stairs from outside. Quite satisfactory provided you remembered that there was a low beam right across the bed about two feet above it.

Lighting for the hotel was by a water turbine, and as the reservoir was silting up a bit, late at night the lights gradually became dimmer and dimmer. However, it must be said that Mr Spratley-Jones was a very good cook, we lived well.

Also at that time I recall hearing on the radio that Stafford Cripps had put a further tax on petrol, making it two shillings a gallon. Petrol is expensive now but in those days, after hearing this news, I really wondered how I was going to afford it.

One of the jobs I had to do for old *"Dolgoch"* (Talyllyn's number 2 locomotive) was make her a new smoke-box door as the original had become paper thin. It was a lengthy and tedious job during which John Snell complained bitterly at having to blow the forge for me. The door must have looked the part as Tom Rolt, in his book *Talyllyn Adventure*, commented on it being 'a good job'!

Attached to the engine shed was a house in which Peter Williams, a retired driver, lived. He passed many a working hour with me, telling me tales of the Railway and Towyn; he was a dear old man and when he had told you some tale one would say, "How long ago was that, Peter?" and he would reply "Oh, not so long ago, not so long ago, maybe thirty years or perhaps forty".

In the spring of 1951 the Talyllyn Railway Preservation Society was able to acquire two locomotives from the neighbouring Corris Railway where they had been standing in Machynlleth yard since 1948. Tom Rolt and I were sent to inspect them prior to their purchase for what was a purely nominal sum.

Just after my arrival the Society acquired, for a nominal sum, two locomotives of the correct gauge from the neighbouring Corris Railway. The first of these, number 3, was built in 1878 by the Hughes Engine Company of Loughborough. The other was number 4, a later engine supplied in 1921 by Kerr Stuart & Co., Stoke-on-Trent. Like *Talyllyn* (the railway's first and number 1 locomotive), number 3 had started life as a 0-4-0 but had trailing wheels added. Whereas number 4, being of later design, was built to a 0-4-2 specification. Both had been standing in Machynlleth station yard since 1948, and when delivered to Towyn, were in very poor condition. The powers-that-be decided to retain their old numbers but changed the names so Number 3 became *Sir Haydn*, and Number 4 *Edward Thomas*.

I immediately set to work on *Sir Haydn* as she was mechanically the better of the two; and I had her steaming by June of that year. She was a nice little locomotive, but the treads on the wheels were subsequently found to be a bit narrow, and the first trip with a train led to several derailments. The method of re-railing was crude, you jacked the loco up and balanced it on a pile of fishplates, when at the right height a push was administered with a bar, and with any luck it fell onto the rails. At the last derailment

We named the two ex-Corris engines ***Sir Haydn*** *and* ***Edward Thomas****. Here we see* ***Sir Haydn*** *in steam for its trial run at Dolgoch with Tom Rolt standing on the left buffer beam (talking to the chief engineer and driver!!) with my wife Barbara on the right-hand platform.*

of the day, well up the line, I was getting somewhat fed-up, furthermore the passengers were a menace, milling around while we were trying to work. Fortunately a large type of wasp started flying around, so I started to beat about, shouting "A hornet! A hornet!" This cleared the deck in a few seconds and I was left in peace to get on and re-rail the locomotive.

But problems with the narrow wheel treads of Number 3 locomotive *Sir Hadyn* persisted forcing us to lay it up, which meant the immediate future of the railway rested upon the services of poor old *Dolgoch*. One day, following yet another

Ex-Corris locomotive Number 3 after her first steam trial in July 1951. Left to right are Tom Rolt, myself and Allan Garraway who later became a key figure in the restoration of the Ffestiniog Railway. (Photo: J.B.Snell).

derailment, Tom Rolt was in the workshop ruefully surveying the damage when a voice from the doorway asked, "Do you mind if I show my small son around in here?" Tom agreed and father and small son entered and wandered around. "What's the trouble?" asked the visitor upon seeing the damaged wheels? When Tom explained what had happened the visitor, obviously an engineer, cast an expert eye over the situation and said, "If you can take the wheels and axles off and get them to my works I can have a new pair of steel wheels pressed for you free of charge." That stroke of good fortune enabled us to put *Sir Hadyn* back into service two weeks later.

Tom and I would wander off in the hot evenings. I remember once above the Dolgoch falls coming upon some wonderful deep pools, we bathed naked with the trout and lay on the grass to dry out.

Another time we went over to Bird Rock. Tom sat on the cliff edge dangling his feet over but I suffer from vertigo and couldn't get within six feet of the ledge.

Barbara helped, acting as guard, but couldn't be there in the holidays as she looked after our adopted son Christopher. They were good times which I look back on with happy memories, particularly as the Talyllyn Railway is now a national institution.

On another occasion a top class British Rail express driver asked if he could have a drive. Thinking he'd be quite proficient we gave him the okay but then he insisted that he burn the small and dusty coal which we normally sieved out, as it was such a waste!

As 6 o'clock came, I did my usual walk outside the shed to look up the line, only to see a few disconsolate people in the distance walking down the line. Oh dear, I'd seen it all before! I wasn't surprised to hear the roar of Tom Rolt's Alvis haring along the road towards the station. A worried Tom alighted, "He got it stuck at Rhydyronen, would you mount a rescue operation and recover the train please?"

I arrived on the scene to find a dead locomotive with no fire, no steam, no water, and fortunately no passengers either! As we were near a stream, I found a bucket, removed a boiler plug, and laboriously walked back and forth, slowly filling the boiler. The fire was nearly out, just a few red hot embers still glowing, so carefully raking out a lot of the hot coal dust. I then routed around in the hedge to procure a pile of dry sticks, prior to sorting out some large pieces of coal. As the fire-box was still hot the fire caught quickly and soon "*Dolgoch*" was hissing nicely, so all that remained was to wait until enough steam had been raised. We had learned through experience that she would only steam on lumps of coal the size of a tennis ball, and larger.

It was getting dark by the time there was enough steam to move, so I lit the oil lamps and slowly set off for Dolgoch station. What a wonderful journey, the odd sheep just caught in the lamp, scuttling for cover, and at last, roars of laughter from Tom waiting on Dolgoch platform. I was certainly ready for a good meal and bed, a rest before collecting the locomotive in the morning and return it to Towyn.

The works at Pendre possessed little in the way of equipment, just a forge, plus an apology for a lathe of which the bed seated on two upturned flat bottom rails. There

This was where all the work was done! The Talyllyn engine shed at Pendre Yard was dark, gloomy and uninviting with nothing much in the way of tools. One of the Kerr Stuart Corris engines can be seen in the process of what turned out to be a lengthy overhaul.

was a total absence of any welding equipment so I bought my own. The workshop was more or less open to anyone so we frequently had visitors—some of which, as previously mentioned, turned into very useful contacts. Also, as one would expect, we had a few strange and weird visitors, one of which was a well dressed young man who just came and stared at us. He never ever spoke or answered if we approached him. Hobbies like this attract all sorts!

Of course Sir Haydn could never lower himself to ask for a boiler inspector to call; in fact I doubt they had any insurance at all. So I had the privilege of putting the serviceable locomotive in order prior to applying for a boiler test. The older of the two locomotives, *Talyllyn*, had been abandoned in an ancient Dutch barn which stood on the site of the new Pendre north carriage shed. I imagined she had been worked to death due to having a better wheel arrangement than No.2 *Dolgoch* with her very wide spacing. I was told, "We only use "*Talyllyn*" in emergency as the boiler is not too good". This was a rather kind way of putting it because a glance into the firebox revealed a large bulge to one side where a stay had pulled out, and the hole was plugged by a standard water plug. There was no way they could have persuaded me to raise steam in her.

No 1 locomotive **Talyllyn** *had been delivered new to Towyn in September 1865 and used in construction of the line. She remained in service until 1946 by which time she was thoroughly worn out and unfit for further use. Fortunately in 1958, after a thorough rebuild at Midland works, she returned to service.*

It was my job to get "*Dolgoch*" through an inspection, assuming it was possible. So I removed the lagging, had a good tap round, did a minor repair on the drain plug fitting and went ahead and called the inspector. He went round everything, asked me to drill a small hole low down in the barrel in order to carry out a thickness check. At $^{5}/_{16}$ inch it was okay so the boiler was passed, it turned out better than expected. However John Snell and I would not have been so happy had we known what would transpire several years later. A tube plate, I think in the smoke-box, was starting to leak, and Hunslets had agreed to repair or replace it, so it was shipped up the works. A few days later Tom received a phone call, saying things were not too good, would he come up and see for himself. Apparently the bottom of the barrel had become corrugated and in parts was very thin, paper thin in fact. Yet around the test plug area, which I had drilled a few years earlier, it remained $^{5}/_{16}$ inch, in thickness–in fact this was one of the thicker parts of the corrugation! Apart from the possible danger, it was a good thing that this did not show itself at the time as the there is no way the railway could have afforded the repairs and it would have been unable to keep going. It also shows how stupidly cautious Health and Safety regulations are now.

I well recall an instance when driving the 'up train' one day. I heard shouting, above the locomotive's general clanking, and looked back to see a coach sideways bumping along on to the track. We were quite used to de-rail jobs, no harm was ever done, but nowadays we would be sued, as some child would be traumatised and need counselling.

My wife Barbara sometimes doubled up as guard and ticket collector. One day a farmer arrived carrying a rake, "How much to take this rake to Rydyronen?" "Sixpence," he exploded, "it only cost two-pence last time!"

I think one of the most hair-raising journeys I ever did was soon after we both arrived and had got old "*Dolgoch*" in steam. We asked the Welsh driver to run us up the track as far as possible. Most of the way, certainly past the winch mechanism at Abergynolwyn, you could not see any of the track at all. We rounded the top bend and looking down to the left, deep into a chasm in the hill, it was possible to see the odd wreck of a slate wagon, plus a pair of wheels, sticking up in the air! I was quite glad to get back to Pendre.

By the top winch were the remains of the hydro-electric generator that supplied the village; if Sir Haydn had any trouble with the quarry labour in the village he just turned the water off, end of argument!

Re-opening of the Talyllyn Railway under Society auspices in Whitsun 1951, with W.G.Trinder cutting the tape for **Dolgoch** *to make the first trip.*

Tom Rolt and I explored the quarry on several occasions. The sheds still retained all of the machinery; goggles hanging on the grindstones seemed ready for the morning shift, the canteen with old newspapers on the table, the workshop with wagon bearings in the vice, and a very substantial manager's house. With a little repair the house would be habitable supplying its occupants with a wonderful view, but sadly it was all inaccessible. Tom drove us up as near as possible using the other side of the valley, it was so steep that going down I had to get out and push down on the tail of Tom's old Alvis car, which only had rear brakes, to stop us sliding off into the valley. Nobody ever ventured to the left of this track as it bordered a deep quarry with shear sides. Chains still hung down the sides and rather spookily clanked in the wind, while at the bottom was a cave which housed a large air compressor for the rock drill. It was an experience never to be forgotten, in fact I am constantly reminded of it by a large Mountain Ash tree which I have in my garden, all those years ago I took a little root from the ground near the compressor. Sadly all the equipment was subsequently sold for scrap.

Before totally concluding my Talyllyn story, in 1953 the Society asked me to build an internal combustion engined locomotive for use during the winter months hauling equipment for track repairs. Tom Rolt wanted me to utilise an ancient Model 'T' Ford petrol-paraffin engine he had removed from the canal boat *Cressy*, but in retrospect this wasn't such a good idea. Furthermore the epicyclic gearbox (also from the boat) proved totally unsuitable for the task in hand. Had I been left to my own devices design-wise I could have provided something more suitable. The Society subsequently purchased a 44-48 hp Ruston & Hornsby which was duly converted to the 2 ft 3 in. gauge and put into service in 1957.

Chapter 9

Formation of Curwen & Newbery

At the end of the summer of 1951 I decided that, having a wife to support, meant taking a more serious view of life. Being on-location at Talyllyn, enjoyable as it was, wasn't exactly financially rewarding, neither did it offer any kind of permanent life-style. Having left Baydon, my wife and I had been living in a rented cottage in Ramsbury, but while staying with my father and mother-in-law at All Cannings, near Devizes, came across a pair of dilapidated cottages in the village and by a stroke of good luck managed to buy them. As I write these memoirs in 2006 we are still living there!

Time for a change in direction, and it was my father-in-law who happened to locate a small general engineers and millwrights business in Devizes, which the elderly owner wished to give up. At the time I was working in a kind of partnership with Edgar Newbery who, fortunately, wasn't short of funds when it came to our various business ventures. He was a charming man who had always wanted to be an engineer but his father never approved. So poor Edgar was relegated into taking over the family business in high class furniture and latterly property, and although it did make money but his heart wasn't in it. When the opportunity to purchase the general engineering business came up, he stepped in and bought it, so we started out as Curwen and Newbery, of Devizes!

Strangely enough we took the business over from a man named Billy Woolrich, a good engineer who loved steam traction engines, having been in charge of them in the army on Salisbury Plain during World War I. He recounted amazing stories of using traction engines to move heavy guns! Being an ingenious engineer he had made a heavy mole plough, and adapted a Fordson tractor with a very heavy winch using a wire rope to pull the plough, which was used for putting in water pipes on farms for irrigation generally in the form of cattle troughs. At the time there was a government grant for this kind of work so we took in on, tackling it when the weather was fine—it was good outdoor work!

With this equipment we were able to install quite a large pipe, 2 inch or so, and I remember one job we did for a small estate on the escarpment near the road to Chippenham. It was a pretty house with lovely gardens, then owned by a Mrs York, whose husband, a gentleman farmer, had been unfortunately killed by the bull. She no longer farmed, and was known to be slightly awkward. In this case we were installing a new main to the house, and I remember we were getting on very well with it. But during the final afternoon I was surprised when Billy started to pack up at only 4.30pm when we were so close to finishing the job. I said we could work on and finish but Billy said, "No, no, if we finish tonight she won't think she has got her money's worth – must come again tomorrow."

Another interesting pipe run was for a farm on a hillside in the village of Seend. If we ran into some shale ironstone we could charge more for the extra work. But this particular shale was full of sea shells! One has to ask how many million years ago did the sea cover this part of Wiltshire. Below in the valley we found the remains of an ironstone working which had been mined at the end of the previous century, but ceased due to transport difficulties.

Another job involved putting a pipe under the Great Western Railway single Devizes to Melksham line. This we did this by digging a hole each side of the track and driving the pipe under with a hefty weight swinging on a rope from a tripod rig.

The G.W.R. insisted we employ their safety man with a red flag and whistle to monitor the work. He wasn't very bright and one day I had to quickly haul him out of the way of a train in order to save his life.

Another line of business Billy Woolrich had developed was the sharpening of lawn mowers and knives. He sharpened knives for several of the town's butchers, and tackled lawnmowers for private customers as well as for Griffins the Devizes ironmongers. Here was a real ironmonger as one knew them from one's youth, a smell of tar, and dozens of little drawers on the wall behind the counter, reaching up to the ceiling. One could buy a box of screws for a few shillings, instead of about three in a little plastic envelope for 10p. It is shops like this that were the basis for the well known sketch in the T.V. programme The Two Ronnies where 'four candles' became confused with 'fork handles'!

Billy had converted an old lathe to grind mower cylinders and each mower, when completed was tested by making it cut a piece of newspaper cleanly. I don't think anyone is that conscientious nowadays! When a mower goes wrong, buy a new one!

At a later date we were approached by Marshall and Fowler to take on an agency, instead of local engineers T H White. Despite the latter's warning we foolishly accepted.. The Marshall tractor, the 'Field Marshall', and the Fowler crawler were fine machines modelled on the hot-bulb Lanz Bulldog – but the snag was, they were expensive in comparison with the Fordson. Furthermore they were tiring for the farmer or ploughman to operate, as the single-cylinder two-stroke with a heavy flywheel, did not damp out the hefty vibration and, although reliable, was not to everyone's liking. They had a 6½ inch bore and one had to be strong to start one by hand. The back of the flywheel had a thread on it onto which you placed a small V-edged wheel; this held the compression release open. You turned the handle as hard as you could, and when the little wheel dropped at the end of the thread you were on full compression, and either it fired, or you were thrown out of the door head first! There was a more humane way of self starting however; you turned the flywheel to the correct position and there was a breach, like a 12-bore gun, which was connected to the cylinder head by a pipe with a right angle to it. You put a special blank 12-bore cartridge in the breach, closed it, and hit the pin with a hammer and bang, you were away. Unfortunately the odd farmer put a 12-bore gun cartridge in by mistake and blew a hole in the pipe!

We never managed to sell the tractor but we did sell a crawler to a farmer in the village where it ploughed on the downs for many years. We sold quite a lot of spares, however, but had to give the agency up and returned the tractor to Marshalls, and here is another story.

When we took the agency on we needed a hefty lorry to take the tractors to demonstrations and to ploughing matches etc. As I have said before, Edgar Newbery was a steam enthusiast, he lived at Aldermaston. Near him at Theale, lived an enthusiast who bought and sold steam lorries, especially Sentinels. So we paid him a visit and bought an S.6. of around 20 tons with a wagon lorry body, of about 1936 vintage, for the magnificent sum of £85. Newbery and I duly presented ourselves to collect it and drive it back to Devizes. Edgar Newbery drove while I fired. It was a good machine, when it had warmed up it trundled along at an easy 50 mph. We got to Marlborough without problem and decided to put our water hose down into the Kennet canal at the bridge behind the College. Here we sucked up a couple of tanks full of water– the tanks were behind the driver and fireman with the fuel bunkers situated on top of the tanks. The chutes brought down the coal or coke just behind your shoulder, so that the dust which filtered out as you ran along gently filtered down your neck!

In hindsight, buying a Sentinel steam lorry wasn't the most sensible of business moves but it was good fun all the same, it is still remembered with some affection around the farming community.

We had just left Marlborough, when Edgar Newbery shouted, "I can't stop! Every time I lift my foot off the brake, the lorry starts off!" I thought maybe the throttle valve had stuck. I could see it situated on the boiler centre low down in the cab so had a look but it seemed to be alright. Then I remembered how the vendor had showed me how to idle the engine to work the compressor and the engine driven water pump. There was a stop valve installed under the cab, to reach it one had to climb partially underneath—quite a risky operation! So I told Newbery to hold his foot on the brake pedal as hard as he could and on no account let it up, as I didn't relish the idea of double tyres of a 20 ton lorry leaving a pattern over my body. He duly did his stuff and I found that vibration gradually opened the valve while we were on route. Closing it remedied the problem and we soon arrived back in Devizes. It was far quieter on the roads in those days!

In hindsight, buying a steam lorry was not the best idea, as it took ¾ hour to get up steam, however painted in orange livery it proved a good advert for the firm. There were times when it was a little unnerving, I remember when returning from a ploughing match on a cold winter evening, I was following the Sentinel in my car. Coming through the village of Lavington, past a rank of thatched houses, a shower of sparks belched out giving me a few anxious moments! If you opened the accelerator violently, a spectacular shower of cinders erupted from the chimney to rain down on the cab roof, and any bystanders!

We had our new tractor to return to the Marshall works at Leeds so I asked two of my employees if they would make the journey using the Sentinel. It took them an incredible four days and was quite an epic journey by all counts.

Having given up our Marshall-Fowler agency we were left with general agricultural engineering, and on this score we made certain machines for Alvan Blanche. These consisted of seed drills and fertilizer spreaders, which were despatched by rail. In those days you just rang up Devizes station and a lorry came and picked and collected whatever machine you needed to despatch. Nowadays there's no station in Devizes and no goods service; how could our politicians have been so short sighted!

We were increasing our manufacturing and sub-contract work which was gradually taking the place of agricultural engineering, pipe laying, and so forth. As the work increased we found we needed larger premises.

The Gas Company had closed the gas manufacturing works in Devizes, and just up the lane from us was the old retort house, in a rather dilapidated state, but a large substantial building. It had been sold to the Council, who now owned it, so we approached them with a view to buying or renting. Things moved very slowly and we sought the help of the local M.P., Mr Potts, but it still dragged on. Mr Hodge, a senior solicitor in the town was Town Clerk, and I remember after such a long delay, visiting him one day to ask if things could be speeded up? He replied that these things just took time and we would have to continue waiting. By this time Edgar Newbery was well and truly fed up; he drew my attention to a builder & contractor, Peter White, who was developing an industrial estate on the grounds of the old flax factory in Devizes, along the London Road.

So in desperation, the two of us went to see Peter who was living in the converted stables of Roundway House. We found him in bed with influenza but, even so, he never missed an opportunity, and within a few minutes he had sold us a plot for a new factory. I cannot for the life of me remember who built it for us but I know the roof trusses were our tubular design and the walls were pre-stressed Charlton Concrete.

It was a very good and clever design. I do not know if this style is still available, but it was thus – a concrete "pot" was sunk into the ground and into each pot the upright stanchions were inserted. These had a grooved channel each side and concrete pre-stressed weatherboard were then slipped in, this pre-stressing was very clever and gave each board strength and elasticity. We had dealt with Charltons before and had inspected the manufacture; several strands of high tensile wire were stretched in the moulds, and concrete poured in, when set and weathered they demonstrated their springiness by standing on a board and it flexed like timber. It made a good cheap building and we never had any bother with it.

Most of our work was of the sub-contract type. We made a lot of moulds for the Avon Rubber Company, also roof trusses, and many parts for various industries. It wasn't long before my favourite type of work came along. Lord Gretton who had two of my 1947/8 Atlantics asked me to build him a replica diesel locomotive, so we built the first of our petrol-engined, diesel style, based roughly on the Great Western Region 'Warship class'.

We also built a 7¼ inch Warship for the Strathavon council; I remember this one very well. The leader of the council, who I seem to recall was named Campbell, came down with two of his assistants. As it happened, I had a loco on hand which I had built for the Gillingham Council in Kent, so they had a look and we talked about it and they asked if I would let them use my office for a council meeting. When they had finished they agreed I should go ahead. Mr.Campbell was totally dressed in black, including his hat, rather like individual in the Sandeman port advertisements. I took them to lunch to finalise things and they drank whisky and a beer chaser – then off back to Glasgow. Some weeks after I rang Mr Campbell, and said, "we are getting on with the loco but I haven't got an official order." His curt reply put me in my place, "Mr Curwen, you have my word, that is enough." In those days a man's word was his bond.

It was a bit difficult to find small petrol engines for these little locos, but we managed to find a twin cylinder air-cooled B.S.A. We used a few others, mostly single cylinder from Villiers or J.A.P. but then Briggs & Stratton took over the market offering very cheap engines in useful sizes up to 15 hp or so, handy for ride-on mowers. And now we have engines from Japan and China, hardly any genuine British examples, yet we were the founders of this market. Another market we let slip through our fingers.

Anyhow, I delivered the engine to Strathavon and ran it in the park for them to see. They had booked me into a

This was the Strathaven 7¼ inch loco with Mr.Campbell driving.

At our new factory in Devizes, I built this replica of a Great Western Region 'Warship Class' locomotive for Lord Gretton (top left) seen here with his son John (lower left) with my engineer Micky Shearing at the rear. I seem to be explaining the intricacies of the modified ignition system!

hotel on the river bank with a wonderful view of the shipyard on the opposite shore, which I suppose is no longer there. Then home – a long journey before motorways.

Lord Gretton's locomotive was built with a four-cylinder O.H.V. car engine (which I seem to recall was of Hillman origin) and we delivered it, staying with his Lordship – Barbara being with me. The locomotive wasn't quite right and it needed a change of gearing, fortunately it was just a question of sprockets and these were available locally. John Gretton, the eldest son, enjoyed helping me carry out this on-sitework.

Lord Gretton had told me previously that they didn't dress for dinner so there was no need to worry! But during the afternoon Lady Gretton said to Barbara "We are having a small dinner party tonight, has your husband brought his dinner jacket?" No worry, I hastily excused myself as I had to work on the loco but I was told to see the butler when I had finished. When I did as instructed, he proffered a nice bottle of champagne!

I rarely refused work, so when Lord Gretton telephoned to ask if I would build a miniature liner to run on his lake, I readily agreed! I subsequently found the lake to be 12 to 18 inches deep in parts!

It was sometime after this that Lord Gretton telephoned saying, "I have an idea – do you think you could build me a miniature liner to run on the lake? The lake is shallow in parts sometimes not more than 12 – 18 inches deep, and I have a drawing and photo of a Shaw Saville liner." In fact they had two of these, *Northern Star* and *Southern Cross*. Being me, I said I thought I could manage it, and got to work with some sketches and details.

This was a 0-4-0 diesel-type locomotive we built for Sir Thomas Salt who used it to drive around his Shillingstone (Nr.Blandford) based estate and feed his pigs! We chose a small Lister LD1 diesel engine for this one which was the first locomotive we built at the old factory behind the court assizes in Devizes.

It was not possible to have a standard screw propeller as the lake was so very shallow, so it seemed to me that a hidden stern wheel could be the answer. Apart from a small boat I had made for myself out of marine ply, I had no boat experience, so I fell back on the only physics experience or knowledge I had gained at school, using the theory of Archimedes. Basically the weight of an article in water displaces that weight of water, which of course it does, so design the boat and calculate the weight and you can find out what its draught would be. I got it about right! When it was launched by a large mobile crane into the water, the draught was eight inches, whereas my own calculations worked out between 7 and 8 inches!

If my memory is right the little liner was 35 ft long, about 8 ft beam, to carry approx 35 to 40 passengers. The Shaw prototype was just right, a small fore deck then a large open play area with the wheelhouse and structure aft.

In the aft superstructure, all the mechanics and stern wheel could be hidden, the engine was a small Ford 4-cylinder, and if memory is correct, it had a paraffin conversion supplied by a firm of maritime engineers on the Norfolk Broads. It used a chain drive to the stern wheel, reversing method I cannot remember; perhaps it wasn't needed as it had only one route, round the island.

After a short trial I excused myself from the official opening, which was a good thing as Lord Gretton had one failing; he was always keen to have his party opening at once, before enough trials were made. This one turned out to be a bit of a disaster. Once all the testing party had climbed on board, away they went across the lake. Gradually the miniature liner got slower and finally came to a halt with engine still running. A most peculiar thing had occurred – when loaded there was not much clearance from the cut-out behind the stern wheel, and thus in revolving, filled the gap with water, working more like a pump, and the stern of the boat just bobbed up and down, sinking a little deeper. Cut the engine, and one could hear the air bubbling out the stern chamber, and the boat rising in the water!

In order to rectify the problem, I took my chief welder

Jack Fell back with me and we carefully cut a larger hole in the stern and higher up – easy really, no more trouble, and it ran for years. We built this miniature vessel in Devizes, and some years later provided a second *Southern Cross* (also for Lord Gretton), this time to my design but built by Severn-Lamb Ltd (model making engineers based in Stratford-upon-Avon), as by then I had resigned from Curwen and Newbury.

It was just before this time that Edgar Newbery who was in his 70's, wanted to retire from the firm so I found a buyer for his shares and we became part of a small group of companies, which were basically a firm of heating engineers. I managed to stay with them for four years, but I find that I can only really work on my own, I always worked best using my own initiative and like to be left to get on with the job in hand. When Edgar finally sold his share in the business, it took me a few months to realise that as he had been the main shareholder which meant I also had been sold as 'the machine that ran things'. After having had my wrong button pressed on several and frequent occasions, it was time to look around for work elsewhere.

I had done quite a lot for the Avon Rubber Co, and had done the odd job for one of their chief engineers Dennis Plowright, who had left the Company and set up as a design consultant working from home. He knew of my unhappiness, and when letting off steam to him one day said, "Why don't you join me?"

This certainly seemed a good idea so I discussed it with my bank manager, Cliff Wilkinson before moving on to the next chapter in my life as an engineer!

Chapter 10

1966 – New Beginnings

I must confess to being unsure about moving on as we possessed little in the way of reserves. However talking to Cliff one day, he said "For God's sake boy take the plunge, I've told you I'll support you, just get on with it." So I took the plunge. Some years after, when he was due to retire, he phoned me and said "I'll have to put a limit to your overdraft before I go just to keep the accounts in order." Apparently I had worked for years with no limit; he just took me on trust.

So the time came and Dennis Plowright and I became associates, we didn't bother with any legal partnership, instead we just looked for an office in Devizes and got on with it. An architect's office came on the market. It was a corner three-storey house in an old part of the town, a rain water down-pipe had a nice cast lead head with 1740 moulded into it. It had originally been an old inn called the Scrabbling Horse, with Sara Paradise the landlady; General Wolfe was supposed to have spent the night there on his way to the coast. It is worth mentioning that a 'scrabbling horse' was a part of the equipment for carding wool, I think combing it with teasels. Anyway we bought it, used the main room on the first floor as our drawing office and Dennis had his office adjoining this, with mine on the top floor above.

We worked together here for quite a few years, designing all sorts of factory equipment. We designed quite a lot of automatic machines for a firm in Swindon, Raychem, that had some special process of ray treatment of plastics which made them shrink when warmed, sleeves that could be put on cables and shrunk tightly – clever stuff, very secret! Dennis did a lot of work with the tanning industry, and I, through a good friend, found a lot of work with the food industry.

My friend Alan Thomsett (along with his partner Lloyd Carter, another clever engineer) ran a company called Ben Nevis in Trowbridge, making egg grading machinery. Alan had been approached by Sainsbury Spillers' chicken factory, to produce certain special equipment. He said he couldn't do this with his commitments but told them he knew a man who could–as they say! That of course was me, so in due course I went up to Bury St Edmunds and talked to their chief engineer, Woodley Jackman. The job they wanted was a rehash of their input of live bird machinery, it was virtually the butchery end of the business, and I had to put all squeamishness well under the table!

The lorries carrying the crates of live chickens came in,

Several jobs came up in the chicken processing industry–rules and regulations are constantly changing rendering machinery redundant virtually overnight!

6 crates high. These were lifted off with a forklift and put on a low trestle from where two or three men then put them on a small conveyor. Another two men lifted out the birds and hung them on an overhead conveyor where they were humanely stunned before being killed. The empty crates were then taken away, put through a washer, and restacked on the lorry. This exercise was pretty labour intensive, about 8-9 men with the supervisor, and pretty heavy work, often requiring spare relief labour. I put my thinking cap on and came up with the following solution.

Six small conveyors each to take a stack of six crates, the fork lift put a stack onto the end conveyor and the stack was then pushed down onto the next conveyor. This went on until all six conveyors were full, then the first stack was pushed into the de-stacker, the platform of this de-stacker immediately rose just above the height of a cage, and the second crate from the bottom was shelf, holding the top five crates. The platform came down with the one crate which was pushed out onto a conveyor, which took it to the two men removing the birds from the crates, the stackers then repeated the operation till it was empty and the cycle started again.

The crates when empty were pushed onto a conveyor which took them through a washer and onto a re-stacker which stacked the crates ready for the fork lift to return them to the lorry.

Everything worked well, but it did mean that every time I arrived at the factory on other business, the first task was to listen to see if it was still working.

Another job I did was for the supermarket group Sainsbury. This entailed a gizzard skinner for removing the interior leathery lining from chicken gizzards– why one was to worry about this item I fail to see, as they are so tough that their only use is for gravy! My memory was of two days spent in the factory among a pile of gizzards trying out the machine. It was a case of sleeves rolled up and chicken fat and meat debris everywhere. The machine was only a partial success.

A firm at Diss took over the manufacture of the stacker system and made a few until the method of using crates was changed. This is a common problem when working for the food industry; outside circumstances, usually entailing new rules and regulations render machinery redundant virtually overnight.

Another firm I worked for was Express Dairies. I was asked to devise a system of dealing with milk crates up to the machine which removed the bottles from the crates. Again the crates came in and out in stacks about 6 high, and were carried on conveyors to a de-stacker and after the bottles were removed the crates were washed and re-stacked. This system was for their depot near Chester and it worked well.

Most of the Express Dairies directors were farmers or landowners, not noted for their generosity. I remember on this contract the factory engineer asked for a gravity conveyor to be power-operated. This was requested at the monthly board meeting where I stated that this would involve extra cost, to which the director agreed asking the head office engineer to make a note of it in the minutes. But when the time came for settlement, they refused to pay the extra. The head office engineer was a decent sort and fed up with this kind of behaviour, so they got me another job in another of their branches to compensate. There was only one drawback to dairy work, it always had to be installed at night and before they started up in the early hours. Cold places, smelling of sour milk, and broken splinters of glass in awkward places – beware!

My associate and I did a job for a local jam factory involving the moving of hot bottles of newly made jam on a conveyor at bench height. On trial, the bottles that did not make it, made a delightful noise when they hit the floor, best description would be "Splat"

As anyone in the food industry will tell you, it is best not be squeamish and close your eyes if necessary. Just tell yourself that the food is safe once cooked or boiled– otherwise you will starve. Take jam for instance, the fruit came in barrels, and looked dreadful, a sort of mud, but when boiled, sugar or whatever added, the end product is excellent. Working with the food industry does have its advantages. I provided a design for Unigate involving the packing and unpacking of butter and was given a gross pack to experiment with. They never asked for it back – it was months before we had to buy any butter.

When you do this sort of work one's wife has to be very forbearing as it means miles of travelling with days away from home. Sometimes Barbara would come with me to make a break and we would spend the night in the Angel at Bury St Edmunds, where for the first time, we had an en suite bathroom, which was quite novel in those days. Sometimes I would leave home at 4 a.m., drive to Manchester, do a days work before leaving to come home at 5 p.m., driving my VW Beetle.

But my real love revolved around the miniature or narrow-gauge locomotives and while I was doing the consultant and design work, I also filled my spare time building these in my home workshop. It was (is !) a hell of a place, terribly untidy, wires everywhere, but comprising a good selection of old machines, bought for a few pounds, from very good friends like Jimmy Wakeham (at the time Managing Director of the Trowbridge branch of Hattersley Newman Hender) , and Alan Thomsett (already mentioned). Jimmy would ring me and say he had a pile of machines due for the breakers, would I like to see if there was anything I would like at scrap price! Of these, a milling machine, drills and two lathes are still working now, converted to single phase.

Way back in the 1960's I was approached by Robin Neville, now Lord Braybrooke, with regard to advising on, and supplying locomotives for, a miniature railway he was intending to build for use of visitors at his Audley End House estate. Apparently he had been in touch with Bassett-Lowke regarding this project and they had suggested he contact me– this was while I was still running Curwen and Newbery, before Edgar Newbery sold his share. A meeting was arranged and Robin came along–usually he drove an XK Jaguar sports coupe or a Bentley with a tinted windscreen–and we talked and talked–just as we continued to do so for the next 40 years, about Railway Locomotives. It came as a great surprise to me when, a few years ago, he asked if I would like to see the first letter I had written to him; the greatest part of the surprise was that, for me, it contained a very good sales pitch!

In the ensuing years I built the following locomotives for him. *Lord Braybrooke* a 2-6-2, *Polar Star* a 4-6-0, *Ivatt Atlantic* a 4-4-2, *Loyalty* a 4-4-0, *Sara Lucy* 2-8-2 (narrow gauge), *Bruce* a 2-4-2 (narrow gauge), *Barbara Curwen* a 2-4-2, *Doris* a 0-6-0 (narrow gauge), *Western Thunderer* (Built by Curwen & Newbury). I'll deal with some of these later but further details of the engines can be found in Lord

Opening Day Ceremony at Audey End in 1964. A rather youthful Stirling Moss leans into the bend while track testing the locomotive, later named, ***Lord Braybrooke****. Although he is looking rather pleased with himself, Stirling was particularly perturbed at the lack of brakes even though I was offering driving instruction from the safety of carriage number 1!*

Braybrooke's excellent little booklet, "*Audley End Railway*", sold in the estate railway shop.

The railway was ready for opening on 16th May 1964 with racing driver Stirling Moss performing the opening ceremony. He was more than a little apprehensive about the brakes when asked to drive a locomotive as the system is far different to that of a racing car. The brakes on a steam locomotive can be classed as a luxury–yes they do the job, but you can always lock the wheels by whacking it into reverse gear providing you don't mind a flat or two on the driving wheels!

Lady Braybrooke driving the Western Class Diesel locomotive ***Western Thunderer*** *built by Curwen & Newbery in 1964. It used a Ford 100E side valve engine coupled to a fluid flywheel from an old Lanchester Ten car. It started off painted in British Rail blue livery but, like so many locomotives, it was at some stage the recipient of a colour change—this time to maroon.*

Of particular interest is a "Diesel Class—Western Region" locomotive I built for (Robin Neville) Lord Braybrooke using a Ford engine mated to a marine type reverse gearbox. To the engine I attached a Daimler fluid flywheel. The drive shaft was fitted with sprockets, a chain driving the gearbox as well as the output shaft, taking the drive to a layshaft in line with the rear bogie. The marine gearbox is equipped with two shafts, the input shaft taking the drive to the output either by a heavy chain, or by two gears meshing. This choice gives you direct by chain, reverse by gears, and selection of which is by a dog clutch. Sounds complicated but it isn't really! We found there was a difficulty in engaging the clutch, because without load the fluid flywheel would creep slightly, meaning the drive shaft would rotate slowly. To remedy this we fitted a small brake to the input shaft, so that the driver could slow things down just enough to engage. The gearing to the rear wheels was all in the bogie using a Ford crown wheel and pinion driving the first pair of wheels while chains and sprockets coupled the other two axles. All this was in a box-like structure in an oil bath, small rollers being supplied for taking up chain wear – which, as became obvious over the years, were simply not required as no wear took place.

For some reason we had to dismantle the bogie some years later, and found that it was quite impossible to get one pair of wheels off, due to fretting which had more or less welded them to the axles. We had to resort to cutting the wheel in two with a torch and re-welded it afterwards prior to re-fitting. This was an interesting point which had occurred on the Kidd rota-flails, and was cured by assembling the shafts and bearings with Molybdenum grease. All this was done with the help of Peter Lewis, who always helped me with these complex feats of engineering.

The other engine was a locomotive we had run at Southend for a couple of years. It had subsequently been laid up on Stephen Brown's farm at Peasmore near Newbury. I told Lord Braybrooke about it and so he went and bought it. I cannot remember if it needed any work done but I don't think it was much, I made it at Baydon in 1948 and it became known as one of the Curwen Atlantics. As so often happens when locomotives change hands, this one had been modified and altered by all and sundry. We steamed it for a test and found that it did not like the steep slope around Lord Braybrooke's Audley End estate, only being in Atlantic guise; I had it back into the workshop and added a couple of driving wheels. This not only involved extending the frames, but replacing the front bogies with a pony truck making it a 2-6-2 Prairie. (I should explain a pony truck consists of one or two axles that together pivot slightly with respect to the engine. They help to bear the weight of the engine, and when placed at the front, provide useful guidance on curves.) This allowed it to take a better load. In doing the modifications the boiler was not long enough by about 10 inches so an extended smoke box was fitted, also

American domes and stove pipe chimney, all castings from the 7¹/4 inch gauge Rio's, more about this later.

Lord Braybrooke was keen to get another steam loco so we built him an Ivatt Atlantic, which was very much a scaled up version of L.B.S.C.'s *Maisie*. An amusing episode occurred when we came to test this engine at the works. An employee, Micky Shearing, was given the major task of building this locomotive and, as with all his work, it was a first class job. However when we came to steam it with pressure up, it wouldn't go! The trouble in this case was that Micky had made a much too good fit of the pistons which were, and still are, light alloy. They were simply too tight and had to be taken out and reduced by a few thousands of an inch, after which everything worked extremely well. However this experience had its ramifications and rebounded on me at a later date, as you will see.

At full steam in the snow! The Rio being driven by Lord Braybrooke who remains hidden under cab which was probably the warmest place on such a day! The fact that the driver can hide his head under the cab clearly illustrates the size of this particular locomotive.

By this time I had built five 7¹/4 inch Rio Grande K.35 2-8-2 locos, so I tentatively suggested to Lord Braybrooke that we should build a 10¹/4 Rio, a real loco? These Rios were Baldwin locos built for the 3 ft gauge and were large powerful machines, with outside frames, wheels inside the frames instead of the usual outside. The full size version hauled heavy mineral trains from the silver mines in Colorado, Silverton to Denver etc. Lord Braybrooke thought it a good idea to build a 10¹/4 version, and so with my usual very minimum of sketches I set to work.

The original 7¹/4 inch Rio, which I will refer to later, was built for Brian Hollingsworth, a very good friend and a steam enthusiast. It was through Brian that the title of this book came about. We were discussing some job or other in my workshop when he asked, "Have you got a rule"? I could not lay my hand on one, it was probably hidden under the usual pile of junk so I happened to say, "Rule, rule – I don't use a rule, what's wrong with my thumb, just one inch?" In a subsequent article he wrote for a magazine he said, "David Curwen just thinks in metal, he gets some and starts cutting it." I had an old works' blue print plus a pile of photos which Brian had supplied, so I made a few sketches to start off the job. I had to make a proper drawing of the boiler as this was an insurance stipulation, plus one had to adhere to British Standard practice. Nowadays we have to work to those awful EU standards, whatever was wrong with the old British Standards? They were excellent and were the forerunners of world engineering. As Tony Benn very sadly remarked on the T.V. when he was at Bristol for the last flight of Concorde – "We had it all and we let it slip though our fingers". One of the saddest things I have ever heard, and politicians are largely to blame, plus banks and accountants, who will not back any project unless it has a computer rating!

For the 10¹/4 inch Rio I had 2 large frames profiled from ³/4 inch steel plate, trued them up with the good old trusty sledge-hammer and set to work. Being in the country I can use a sledge-hammer without hindrance if I'm careful. Unlike the last inexperienced factory inspector we had some years ago in Devizes. He arrived when one of my employees happened to be bending some heavy plate with heat and a hammer, the young inspector came to me and said, "That's rather noisy, can't he use a rubber mallet!"

When building an outside frame loco I found that one had a readymade ball bearing axle-box, by using standard self-aligning plummer block bearings, and cutting the top of the casting. This was a very good and cheap way of doing it because with outside wheels you cannot get the bearings on. A few years ago, visiting another maker of narrow gauge locos, I found they had also used the system, presumably from seeing some of mine, I should have patented it.

The loco building progressed apace, and on this one I was persuaded to use Loctite 'Shaft Fit' for the first time. I had cast the balance weights in cast iron; or rather Vernon Bull had cast them for me in his foundry. I machined these and took them for pressing of the crank pins to a firm in Radstock which had a 100 ton press. All went well until the last one – the operator said "It's a bit tight, shall I go on?" "Please..." and there was a crack like a rifle shot! Consequently one new weight had to be made. I was about to start when I had a visit from Bill Winter, a first class engineer who had a firm at Colerne. He said, "Why on earth don't you use Loctite? Here, I'll show you" Giving it 3-4 thou clearance, he put the pin in, and it's never moved since.I also used it later on the pony wheels as one didn't go quite home by ¹/16 inch. I could never move it and it has lasted the 20 years until a major rebuild recently.

As with most 'hands-on' engineers, most of my locos have left some scars on my person. With the Rio, it was a six inch U-shaped mark in pure white on my left forearm! I was forging a coupling rod when the bar I was using slipped; the end of the rod was red hot and came into contact with me.

One of several 'Western' Class 10¼ inch gauge diesels I designed for Severn-Lamb Ltd using a choice of mechanical or hydraulic drive. ***Western Comet*** *was another locomotive to start life painted in a shade of blue only to be the subject of a colour change at some stage in its life. This one, at the time of going to press, was the subject of an extensive wheels upward rebuild by Joe Nemeth Engineering.*

With my wife at Ludlow in the 1970s. I've included this picture to illustrate that engineers do go on holiday, and can dress for the occasion when required!

I had a nice flap of cauterized arm to push back into place and strap with Molomine plaster. A good doctor friend who came each week for a meal was shown the damage; his verdict was – "leave it if it's clean and cauterized" – and leave it I did.

As my story is told roughly in chronological order I must briefly leave locomotive construction at this point in order to include details of a somewhat unprofitable, although enjoyable excursion I made into the realms of internal combustion engineering. However before doing so I should mention a design for a 'Western' Class diesel locomotive I made for Severn-Lamb Ltd using a choice of mechanical or hydraulic drive. Of the several produced the example shown in the photograph used a Ford 105E engine, a fluid flywheel and hydraulic drive. Sadly, in the interest of simplifying construction the builders departed from my original design by squaring off the front corner between the side-glass and windscreen, a point often picked up by sticklers for originality! It is re-assuring to know that so many engines built to my designs are still in existence; I was lucky enough to see *Western Comet* undergoing an extensive rebuild at Joe Nemeth Engineering in 2006.

Chapter 11

Hartop Interlude

The idea of constructing a small-power stationary engine occurred while visiting my friend and great authority on stationary engines Charles Hudson, who at that time lived in Sussex. On the way home I put together a plan, bearing in mind I had never attempted to deviate from the realms of external combustion before, so dabbling with internal combustion would be an entirely new venture. Charles thought the Hartop AV would be a suitable candidate for the project based on the fact that he was in a position to supply a complete engine from which to make plans. Furthermore he was in contact with Thomas A Hartop, who at the time resided at Clacton-on-Sea, so from this source Charles was able to obtain a complete set of drawings for both the 1¼ hp and the diminutive ½ hp AV types. For ease of production I made just two alterations departing from the original, by adding a balance weight on the crankshaft, and spur gears instead of skew gears, as later used by Hartop.

My venture into the realms of internal combustion engineering was short-lived with a Hartop type AV Replica of which only five were completed. It had a 3⅛ inch bore x 4 inch stroke, supplied 1½ hp at 600 rpm and weighed 1½ cwt. Colour scheme was black, green or reddish brown. The price in 1975 was rather high at £175-00p plus VAT, tested and ready to run. Sadly the project was a labour of love!

Next job involved producing a set of patterns and in these I was lucky in that I possessed a curved spoke flywheel of the correct diameter but just a little heavier. From this I had an aluminium pattern cast and a set of castings turned out from the foundry which I used to make my steam engine parts.

I only made one of the ½ hp size Hartop but am currently in the process of machining another set of castings which I happened to find under a bench!

It was a very straightforward engine with a wet liner held in place with the cylinder head and while the original seals were asbestos for packing, I used a standard 'off the shelf' easy to find 'O' ring. The crankshaft was a fabricated and welded construction, being trued after manufacture; the connecting rod was fabricated steel unlike the originals which were sometimes cast bronze and occasionally broke. A suitable Amal carburettor was found while the magneto was a Lucas SR, both being hard to source and probably even harder today!

This whole project turned into a very expensive exercise; I only made five of the 1¼ hp size and one of the ½ hp and sold them at a price which only just covered the cost of the materials used. The last example currently resides with my good friend David Edgington, which reminds me of another rather amusing incident.

For a test run and initial evaluation I took a complete engine to Westbury to the home of David Edgington who was at that time editor of *Stationary Engine Magazine*. Charles Hudson who was also in attendance, rigged it up to run on a workbench and rather wisely asked David to do the honours with the starting handle. The engine coughed and fired first swing, kicking off the handle which forcibly collided with David's forehead knocking him to the floor, much to the amusement of Charles Hudson. To this day David still has a lump on his forehead as a reminder of that occasion!

Chapter 12

Polar Star, Loyalty and Barbara Curwen

Polar Star *4-6-0 No. 4005, built in 1989, took longer to build than any other of the Curwen steam projects, all four cylinders are a little cramped inside.*

Returning to the locomotive theme, the next project was *Polar Star*, a G.W.R. Star class loco for which we got a set of 5 inch gauge drawings. It was built as per prototype, as a four cylinder engine. A fine-looking locomotive, but not one for earning its keep on a small railway as the internal valve gear is, to my mind, too complicated and rather too light. This type of construction was however a necessity because of the limited room between the frames. Daily hard work would mean packing glands etc on the inside cylinders and valves, and trying to carry this out without removing the boiler would be difficult. It also has a very long narrow firebox, not easy to fire. I have always maintained that for ease of operation on a miniature railway which has to pay its way, a wide firebox is essential; plus outside motion and valve gear, with as large cylinders as possible, so that you can get at everything, and you are still able to pull a good load if the pressure is a bit down.

The *Polar Star* is the only loco I have made with piston valves and they gave me so much trouble that in the end I used Henry Greenly's modified valves which worked satisfactorily.

As I've already mentioned, most engineers probably carry 'body damage' which can be attributed to various projects, but the only damage to my person from *Polar Star* happened when it managed to nip the tip off my little finger when I was turning the chassis over. A lady doctor, at Devizes hospital, sewed it back on for me, as simple as that!

Then there was *Loyalty*, an L.N.W.R. Precursor made using a set of 5 inch drawings I managed to obtain. It had balanced slide valves which worked well and Lord Braybrooke uses it as his personal loco. It is not in regular personal use but it is very fast. I thought I was being clever

On the test bed! The designer/builder in his grubby workshop using compressed air to test ***Polar Star*** *by placing rollers under the driving wheels. Nowadays Health & Safety would definitely not approve of this method, especially if I said I had chopped off a small piece of my finger!*

trying to do a modification on the tender, fitting a fibreglass inside instead of my usual rubber skin made with motor-car under-seal. It was a disaster and I had it back and under-sealed it. I had real problems with the tender and have to say a 'Curwen tender', just a square box, is best! I find if a loco is of my choice and my design I can build it in about 2 years. If to someone's drawings, and as per prototype, you can at least double this!

Take the axle boxes alone. *Polar Star's* were most complicated, many machining operations, too expensive gunmetal castings. Compare this against the Rio and No. 24 using standard commercial ball-bearing assemblies, all easy to buy locally.

No. 24 was a fairly straightforward job, a plain and rather hefty loco for pulling good loads; I felt she was very right for the job.

And then came *Barbara Curwen* built to use up a spare boiler left over from the rebuild of the Curwen Atlantic which is now called *Lord Braybrooke* – it was originally, for reasons totally unknown, named *Gordon*. *Barbara Curwen* came after *Blanche* and *Linda* of the Festiniog, a Hunslet. She was at first like her namesake, difficult at times, but this has been ironed out and now she is Steve the driver's favourite locomotive.

One of the quickies was *Doris*, made up of bits and pieces such as an old Morris front wheel drive engine and gearbox, with various chains and sprockets. She is a good workhorse, and would be classed, in railway terminology, as the "shed engine", pulling things in and out, shunting and doing

Loyalty *is Lord Braybrooke's personal loco, it is exceptionally fast and consequently restricted to owner-driver!*

Barbara Curwen, *the last of my heavier locomotives and a favourite with driver Stephen who runs the Audley End Railway. It gave us some bother when first made—just like its namesake at home! I was in my mid 80s when this task was completed in 1997.*

the odd service job. She was rather noisy with a full cab, vibration causing drumming, but the people operating it cut off its roof off, rather drastic but that cured it!

In my opinion Lord Braybrooke should have been an engineer! In all my engineering life very few people who I have worked with, understand that if you are making, or just designing, an individual machine you must expect to have teething troubles. Maybe a lot of people do understand this and take great pleasure in finding fault. Not so with Robin (Lord Braybrooke), he has understood this from the start, with nine locos there have been problems all of which have been taken with understanding and with more good grace than I should have given myself. We have never fallen out as far as I can remember. It has all been very worthwhile.

I completed **Doris** *in 1982, she is powered by an Austin 1100 engine and gearbox mounted east-west across the frame. In railway terminology she would be the 'shed locomotive' used for general out-of season work shunting rolling stock and 'dead' locomotives around. Steve Crow (seen here), is Lord Braybrooke's engine driver and general factotum at Audley End while wife Sandra runs the estate bookshop. Photo by Alan Thomsett.*

By the time I had reached my late 80's, Lord Braybrooke saw that heavy work was getting a bit much for me and the idea was spawned to build a private scenic line in Abbey House garden, something you could take a glass of whisky to a chair and watch it go round. As he already had a few very nice 5 inch gauge locos we decided upon a 5 inch gauge track. A specialist was brought in as a layout designer and builder and I have to admit it has turned into a very attractive feature. The Estate carpenter made a very nice station while I made an over-bridge, and a building for the other platform, also a signal box made with miniature bricks which gives it an uneven texture. It would have been easier to make it in 3 ply and cover it with thin brick tiles, which I finally used on the station building, also there was an 8 foot bridge all in steel, signals many of them, station lamps etc. Rolling stock consists of some 15 wagons of different types,

You could be forgiven for thinking this picture depicts a busy main line railway with a diesel locomotive rushing past a signal box. In fact this is Lord Braybrooke's 5-inch gauge railway! I built the diminutive signal box at home using bricks $\frac{7}{8}$ inches long by $\frac{1}{4}$ inch wide.

2 guards vans, tank wagon, ballast wagons. Of course I let myself in for a lot of work by suggesting a cement wagon which was discharged by compressed air requiring one mass of strengthening stiffeners. As all the wagons were for scenic work and look good going round, a lot of the detail was bypassed. I also made a Kerr Stewart diesel shunter, electric drive, very simple belt drive but works well and can be brought out at a moment's notice. A nice touch as far as I was concerned due to the previously explained family connection, my father-in-law being Kyrle Willans who was the designer of this locomotive when he ran Kerr Stuart.

After leaving Curwen & Newbery and setting up with ex-Avon Rubber Co., engineer Dennis Plowright, we looked around for any suitable design work. I picked up a job building the first Rio in $7\frac{1}{4}$ gauge for Brian Hollingsworth. Brian was a charming quiet chap who loved steam engines and he and I got a lot of fun getting this project off the ground.

Then there was the Dobwalls Railway of John Southern, he had a pig farm but wanted to start a railway and had bought a very nice $7\frac{1}{4}$ gauge *Duchess of Sutherland.* I made him a diesel type G.W.R., I think a Warship Class, using an old 500 cc Fiat engine of pre-war vintage, later he sold it and I don't know what became of it but expect it is still around somewhere.

I was building another $7\frac{1}{4}$ inch Rio for a young man living near Winchester whose father had a very nice plastics factory making precision plastics like O-rings. But before the loco was finished the lad gave up the idea of having a railway and asked if I could find a buyer, so I got in touch with John Southern and persuaded him to buy it. This was really the best advice I could give John and although he would not give me credit this was the start of his success. A good model of a British loco in $7\frac{1}{4}$ inch gauge is really too small in all its working parts to last for years on the sort of very hard day to day work of a public railway. But a small American loco, on a 3 ft gauge, is a big loco for $7\frac{1}{4}$, about equal to a $10\frac{1}{4}$ British loco, and being a hefty piece of work with 4 inch bore cylinders is a sound work horse. Subsequently I made him another Rio, plus a small 2-6-0 or Mogul, a simple loco, with either Hackworth or a modification of Hackworth valve gear. John used aluminium track, I tried to persuade him to go steel as the softer metal wears wheels like nobody's business, but he wouldn't; consequently I had to do a very major overhaul on the Rio which included shrinking on tyres on all 20 wheels. John, who was not mechanically minded, had no idea how much work and hours were involved by Peter Lewis and me and sadly we fell out over the bill!

I built one or two other small locos of the narrow gauge industrial type, one for Mr Pritchard of Peco, who concentrated on 00 gauge tracks and track-work, never on

I also built this portable 'farm engine' as an interesting project for Charles Hudson. It has a 12 inch diameter firebox boiler and was particularly nice to watch ticking over!

locomotives, and it's on the locos you can come up against trouble. Another was *Brock* for James Boyd (who was a member of Talyllyn Society's Council, and later became a well-known author) who lived at Colwall and this was for the Colwall school railway. It had been Boyd's prep school, and living nearby, he kept in touch. I first heard of this railway via the *Model Railway News* when I was at my prep school—which had no railway, and wondered why my parents should have overlooked such a detail! I made a little diesel shunter in 7¼ inch for Charles Hudson who, at the time was helping with the formation of the Amberley Museum. Behind Charles's house (in West Chiltington) he put down a track around the perimeter of a field, and housed a couple of locomotives in domed terminus 'garages' which he had grassed over. From the rear they resembled grassed hillocks. When he gave up his business revolving around horticultural machinery repairs, I bought the open crank 10 hp Ruston & Hornsby stationary engine and alternator set-up he had used to power his workshop. I planned to set it up as a standby plant but found the task of swinging the starting handle too onerous, however I still have it and still have plans–one always does! However, Robin (Lord Braybrooke), gave me a Lister CS Start-O-Matic set which came from the Audley End estate. These sets are far easier to use and this one starts and runs well and is ideal in times of power cuts.

We have wandered again from the Railways, so back. We made several later type Western Region diesels, all using Ford 8 or 10 hp engines, except one which we made for the Margate Pier and Harbour Board, this had a 3 cylinder diesel engine and has just come to light again, as it has been bought by Peter Bowers whose Royal Victoria Railway at County Park, near Southampton will be running it; he also runs *Isambard Kingdom Brunel* I made for Peter Webb of Penzance.

Even at 93 years of age I can still start my Lister CS powered 230-volt Start-O-Matic standby when we have mains failure. It is a 1960s 6hp diesel, one of a pair coming from Audley End Estate. It provides an easy 2½ kW which is enough for one's immediate needs.

Chapter 13

The Age of Steam

It is surprising just how many people harbour an ambition to build a small railway, a desire probably stemming from childhood! And, like so many other hobbies, this one has a tendency to attract people who enter with the greatest of ambitions only to suffer from waning enthusiasm. Others are forced to move on simply due to unforeseen, or unfortunate, circumstances. Take Peter Webb, for instance, who managed to get a very good site for a proposed railway near Penzance at an old mine working. Although the site was uneven, making building and track laying more difficult, it was much more interesting for visitors. Unfortunately for Peter and his wife Iris, as soon as they had started on construction the weather turned awful and everything was held up and cost twice as much. He had bought a locomotive from Marsh, it was a rather odd-looking narrow gauge example; anyway he asked me to build another tender locomotive of a different type, a Mogul, the track was 10¼ inch gauge. Although it performed well but I seem to remember there were some clearance problems in the tunnel or perhaps it was a rather too sharp radius. It was really a nice little Theme Park and Peter had plans for holiday chalets running down to the chine near the sea, but sadly planning permission was refused and it all went wrong and finally closed. I recall having problems recovering stock I had loaned for his museum, but the worst of it was the new owner actually obtained the necessary planning permission!

Building engines from bits and pieces is a task to be avoided! This engine was intended for an ex-naval vessel belonging to a Dr.Stevens who had bought it as a restoration project. In the end it would have been far easier to design and build an engine from scratch than to be given the task of 'working in' existing parts. Dr.Stevens sold the boat and I believe it is still in the Wiltshire area on the canal somewhere. Perhaps someone will recognise it?

Seaside resorts are always popular for miniature railways. I made another of the Western Region type diesel replicas for Mr and Mrs Pugson of Minehead who owned a café and gift shop on the sea front. They owned a nearby piece of land near, where they put up a 10¼ inch circular railway run by just the one locomotive, no steam on this one.

I was contacted by Douglas Ferriera of the Ravenglass & Eskdale Railway, for whom I designed and built a few bogies for their carriages. While up there one day I was shown the start of a diesel loco that their charming old engineer Tom Jones had begun constructing, but due to work pressure had been unable to complete. So Douglas asked me to produce a design which I did, using a hydraulic drive, the construction work going to Severn Lamb. We used a new German hydraulic system, a Linde, and upon the delivery trial the loco performed well. But two days after delivery, I got a phone call – "won't go" – so Peter and I went up and found the hydraulics were providing very little pressure.

I came back and rang the firm near Bristol who had very kindly introduced me to the Linde which they used on heavy paint stirring equipment they made. They told me at once that they had just had similar trouble, which was due to strike trouble at the Linde factory. Sand had either been deliberately put into the pumps or had not been cleaned out of the castings. Linde came up trumps and supplied replacements, so all ended well. *Sheila* of Eskdale is, I believe, still running today.

One day I had a phone call from yet another person interested in building a railway. His name was John Ellerton.

This is the marine boiler I designed to go with the engine I made for Dr.Stevens using cylinders and other parts he had found. I always preferred to source my own parts!

He had a French wife, and they had big plans for a railway in France. Here's a lesson—never judge your future client from a telephone conversation. He had an American accent and turned up dressed as a cowboy, very smart but not what I expected! I suggested either a $10\frac{1}{4}$ or 15 inch gauge simply because parts were easy to find–and there would be many of them, but John being John decided on $12\frac{1}{2}$ inch so $12\frac{1}{2}$ inch it was. He asked John Milnes to build him a Darjeeling loco, and he gave me an order to build a small version of *Lyn*, the Lynton and Barnstaple loco, and later an order for a copy of *Beddgelert* built by the Vulcan Foundry in 1877 for the Welsh Highland Railway.

Finally the copy of the Lynton and Barnstaple locomotive *Lyn* was finished and sent off to France. We had one minor mishap when loading. Instead of the requested low loader, a standard height lorry turned up, so we put up a piece of rail onto the tailboard and using a wire hand winch, hoisted it up just to the point of balance when the wire broke! Fortunately there is a soft earth bank behind and the loco ran into that; no damage done but it was dark before we retired, somewhat fatigued.

So we set off to France in Peter's van, leaving from Portsmouth. When we arrived we found the French Customs would not release the locomotive so we had to do battle for three days in order to acquire it. I even had to befriend the local mayor in order to speed things along. We were quite a party, Peter, Lord Braybrooke, Geoffrey Barrett, and dear old Vernon the foundry owner who had made all the castings for me. John Ellerton had supervised all the track laying; I think it was about 7 miles of it. The only trouble was on some of the roads crossing it, there wasn't enough clearance, and on our first trip the back buffer beam got very bent, hitting a proud rail end. Finally we managed to iron all the snags out and enjoyed a run or two, and very much enjoyed the little hotel and its food. Gradually all my party had to go their various ways, and as I had a bit more to do, dear old Vernon Ball said he would stay on with me. I well remember our last dinner together, I went to the proprietor and said, as it was our last dinner, would he prepare a rather special meal, complete with wines?

He was delighted, we had to see his beautiful stainless kitchens and the meal was wonderful, he only charged an extra franc for it, too.

Chapter 14

The best steam engine I have ever seen!

As previously mentioned, I carried out a lot of work for the Stratford-on-Avon firm of Severn-Lamb. One day Peter Lamb telephoned to ask if I had any idea as to where a Willans Central Valve steam engine could be located as the Smithsonian Institute had asked him if he could find one. I didn't know of one so telephoned my brother-in-law Bill Willans (Peter Willans grandson) and immediately picked up a lead. Apparently King Edward V11 hospital in Midhurst possibly still had one that had been withdrawn from service a while back. I immediately made contact and received a letter from the Clerk of Works saying they had two Willans engines which they were in the process of selling for scrap for £100 the pair! Fortunately preservation always takes precedence over scrap so we were able to snatch them from such a cruel end in the nick of time. Peter Lamb and I went to see them and found two engines in first class condition plus the foundations of what had been a third. Apparently the only reason for parting with them was that they had D.C. generators, which were an integral part of the base casting, and could not be converted to A.C. The engineer, assuming we would like to see one run, turned on the steam and brought the engine slowly, and silently, into life. Its operation was almost silent; the only noise was from the hum of the dynamo. By pressing one's ear against the cylinder wooden lagging it was just possible to hear a faint tick, tick, tick! Peter took a penny coin out of his pocket and stood it on edge on the top of the cylinder where, amazingly, it didn't topple over; there was no vibration at all. That's what I call a real engine, the best I have ever seen.

The definitive high-speed Willans engine type was of central-valve operation like this 3-cylinder version–my brother-in-law Bill Willans is seen here on the left. Lubrication was by the "splash" system, with the cranks dipping into the oil at the bottom the crankcase, which was therefore enclosed to prevent oil splashing everywhere. They ran smoothly at 350 to 500 rpm, and were highly successful in the emerging electricity supply industry. In 1895, the installed capacity of British power stations was about 100,000 horsepower, 53,000 of which were produced by Willans engines.

The sets were about 80 kW, eight to ten feet high, 2-cylinder triple expansion. The third engine had, over the years, been dismantled as a source of on the spot spares, and believe it or not, everything interchanged.

My father-in-law Kyrle Willans had previously told me that his father Peter Willans was a real stickler when it came to accuracy, and would walk up a line of finished engines, carefully examining and measuring each one–any slight errors would render the engine as scrap. Peter Willans said there was a limit on the horse power because of the system of splash lubrication employed; speed was limited to 450 rpm.

Bellis & Morcom subsequently made a more powerful and faster engine by pumping oil through the crankcase and bearings under pressure. I feel sure, had Peter Willans lived, he would have done likewise, but at the age of 42 he was killed by a pony bolting and throwing him out of his trap on the way to the factory.

Chapter 15

Making a locomotive!

We've now reached 2006 and at 93 years old it would be easy to say I've had enough but that would be a defeatist attitude as there is still much work to do. My workshop, as the picture clearly shows, resembles a well used museum of engineering with antiquated machinery, the odd cob-web, and endless off-cuts of metal, the residue of countless jobs undertaken over several decades. In this workshop tons of steel, copper and brass have been painstakingly turned into locomotives that have given pleasure both to their owners as well as thousands of people, and children, who have travelled as delighted passengers.

So in conclusion I though you might like to be taken through the procedure involved in the construction of a locomotive…

Initially it is essential to know if the locomotive is intended for public use, ie. the earning of money for its owner. Certain types are better placed for this type of use, being easy to start and run, easy to maintain and using commercial parts that can be bought as replacements off the shelf. On the other hand if it is to be a locomotive that the client particularly likes, and not intended as a money earner–such as Lord Braybrooke's *Polar Star* and *Loyalty*, with their narrow fireboxes,–then it is a different matter. Engines for private use, like the two mentioned, are far more difficult to build. For each one I worked to a set of drawings supplied and they took much longer to construct—probably 4 to 5 years. There are many complicated parts to make, such as the axle boxes for *Polar Star* which required a multitude of machining operations—so unlike my own outside frame engines using standard bearing races and off the shelf, easy to source, components. I have to admit to being a complete heathen—I just don't like working to drawings! I was asked to design an engine (to be built by Berwyn Engineering) for use on the well-known, Wiltshire based, Longleat Estate and it took me two months just to make the drawings for an engine to be built by someone else! What an utter waste of time, when all that is needed are just a few dimensions, perhaps sketches of cylinders etc. to make sure the various moving parts will have enough clearance.

The boiler is a different matter; this must be drawn out fully as it needs to be approved by an insurance firm and checked out by their appropriate engineers. This of course is time consuming and expensive especially with 21st century rules and regulations. The old engineer/inspectors, most strangely enough of Scottish descent, who used to approve and stamp my drawings for nothing, sadly no longer, exist. What an extensive knowledge of steam they possessed; nowadays it would be hard to find such characters.

So let's look at the procedure involving in making a locomotive from scratch. The first task is to study photographs and, if possible, a detailed dimensional drawing of the type of locomotive you want to build. Take for example the first one I built for Brian Hollingsworth. He wanted a 7¹/4 inch gauge *Rio Grande* 2-8-2 to run on a 3 ft gauge tack. This was an ideal locomotive. He gave me some photographs he had taken, plus a line-drawing, and an erection drawing he had obtained. So from this material it was easy to scale down the various components to size.

Of course the first job is the woodwork, making the patterns for the cylinder assembly and other parts requiring casting such as chimney and dome etc. For an outside frame locomotive, blank steel discs can be used for wheels, so no

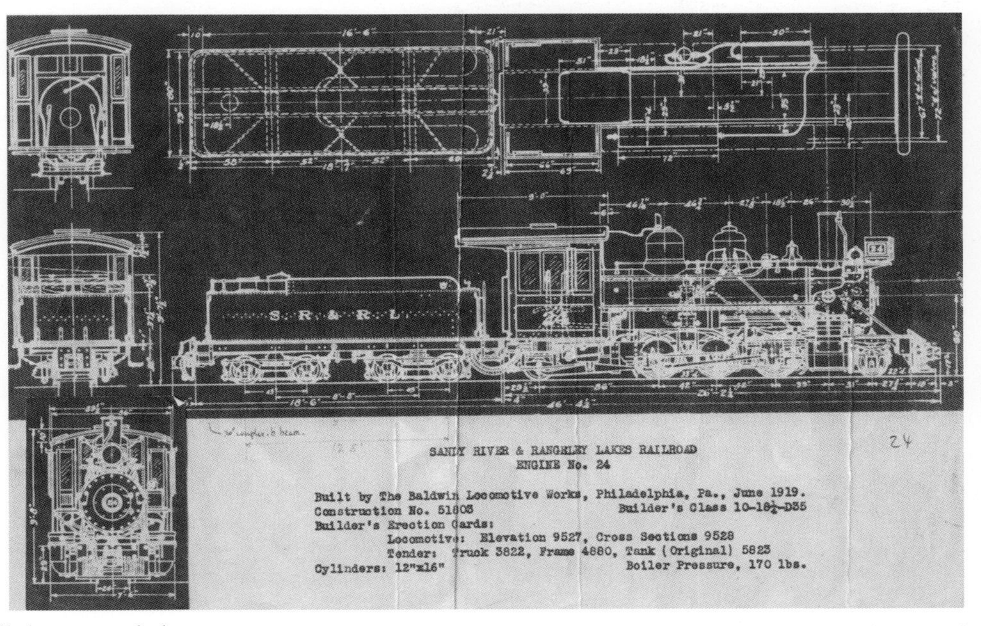

Sometimes a prospective customer would present me with a set of plans—like these for a 1919 Baldwin 2-6-2.

complicated spokes needed. I should just explain that an outside frame means the wheels are concealed inside the main frames so are not visible from the outside. If they should be positioned outside you will need special axle boxes, which will fit over the axles, behind the wheels which have been fixed to the axles. But with the frame outside the wheels the axle protrudes outside the wheels making life much easier as many standard parts can be used.

The first job is to make the frames. I would draw these out, being sure to get the dimensions correct, and then find a good firm who can profile them with acetylene cutting equipment. Getting this is done accurately means there would be little machining or filing to do afterwards, thus saving time and effort. As American locomotives have bar frames I find it is possible to fake these by having them cut from thick plate, either 5/8 or 3/4 inch, good old English dimensions. I do not fix the cylinders as they are usually done in bar frames, so I end the bar part of the frame just behind the portion of the cylinders. Then I revert to the standard of British plate frames with cylinders bolted to the plates' angle-iron buffer beams with suitable angle brackets to fix them to the frames. Then frame spacers are fitted, as and when required, but bearing in mind the mounting for the smoke-box also forms a spacer.

When it comes to valve gear it is entirely up to what the client requires. Walschaert is usual but Baker (Walschaert's main competitor) is also very good and doesn't have a curved link which requires a jig for machining.

Now is a good time to pause to take a good look at the photographs or drawings and pick out a certain feature that really stands out. Remember you need a locomotive that really looks nice in front of the general public. The American Baldwins had stays from the smoke-box to the buffer beam—they don't do anything for strength on your smaller machine but leave them off and it doesn't half look naked, and oddly enough, far less powerful. Also if you are perhaps building a more modern looking diesel engine and it has rounded corners to the cab, don't have sharp right-angles instead. It may be easier to build this way but it will surely spoil the end result. A firm I did some design work for, made both of these mistakes and in doing so spoilt both locomotives—the public may not have noticed, but I did! Here's a further observation which may sound obvious. If you are building a large locomotive, don't make a scale cab or footplate otherwise you might not fit inside it! Get a board or two, and a brick or two, and make yourself comfortable, then measure up all around so you will fit—a few inches here or there won't make much difference or look out of place. And another tip, sink a well for your feet in the footplate area as there is usually plenty of room. These creature-comforts make a lot of difference and make good sense if a locomotive is going to be used throughout the year and for several decades. I would set aside two to three years to build an own-design locomotive with up to five years for a specialist job.

Looking back through forty-years of locomotive design and building, it was working for Lord Braybrooke that gave me the most pleasure. We always had great fun discussing the planning stage of each project, furthermore he always understood the work involved and wasn't at any time dismayed when we experienced a few teething troubles during test runs. I attended the 40th anniversary of his Audley End railway in May 2004 and it was such a pleasure to see the subjects of my hard work steaming around his track.

When I look at the *Rio*, the largest of my locomotives, I wonder how on earth I managed to make it using my old and clapped-out machine tools, but as Brian Hollingsworth once said, "David Curwen thinks in metal, he just starts cutting it"

Here I am just in the final process of assembling the valve gear linkages on ***Rio Grande*** *in about 1976, in preparation for a test run and completion the following year. Photo by Alan Thomsett.*

Working in a time-warp! In 2006 the old workshop, used in the construction of around twenty-five locomotives and countless other engineering based projects, is still in use. Some people are amazed when I say I am still using a 1913 Drummond lathe–"but its 93 years old", they say. Well so am I !!!!!